W9-AVC-299

YA 980 LATIN AMERICA
Latin America : opposing
viewpoints
b]
1143413612
WITHDRAWN
by
JEFFERSON COUNTY
PUBLIC LIBRARY, CO

JEFFERSON CO PUBLIC LIB, CO

Latin America

Other Books of Related Interest:

At Issue Series

Foreign Oil Dependence

The U.S. Policy on Cuba

Current Controversies Series

Homeland Security

Opposing Viewpoints Series

Free Trade

"Congress shall make no law ... abridging the freedom of speech, or of the press."

First Amendment to the U.S. Constitution

The basic foundation of our democracy is the First Amendment guarantee of freedom of expression. The Opposing Viewpoints Series is dedicated to the concept of this basic freedom and the idea that it is more important to practice it than to enshrine it.

Latin America

Louise I. Gerdes, Book Editor

GREENHAVEN PRESS
A part of Gale, Cengage Learning

Detroit • New York • San Francisco • New Haven, Conn • Waterville, Maine • London

GALE
CENGAGE Learning™

Christine Nasso, *Publisher*
Elizabeth Des Chenes, *Managing Editor*

© 2009 Greenhaven Press, a part of Gale, Cengage Learning

Gale and Greenhaven Press are registered trademarks used herein under license.

For more information, contact:
Greenhaven Press
27500 Drake Rd.
Farmington Hills, MI 48331-3535
Or you can visit our Internet site at gale.cengage.com

ALL RIGHTS RESERVED.
No part of this work covered by the copyright herein may be reproduced, transmitted, stored, or used in any form or by any means graphic, electronic, or mechanical, including but not limited to photocopying, recording, scanning, digitizing, taping, Web distribution, information networks, or information storage and retrieval systems, except as permitted under Section 107 or 108 of the 1976 United States Copyright Act, without the prior written permission of the publisher.

For product information and technology assistance, contact us at

Gale Customer Support, 1-800-877-4253
For permission to use material from this text or product, submit all requests online at www.cengage.com/permissions

Further permissions questions can be emailed to permissionrequest@cengage.com

Articles in Greenhaven Press anthologies are often edited for length to meet page requirements. In addition, original titles of these works are changed to clearly present the main thesis and to explicitly indicate the author's opinion. Every effort is made to ensure that Greenhaven Press accurately reflects the original intent of the authors. Every effort has been made to trace the owners of copyrighted material.

Cover image copyright Gary Yim, 2009. Used under license from Shutterstock.com

LIBRARY OF CONGRESS CATALOGING-IN-PUBLICATION DATA

Latin America / Louise I. Gerdes, book editor.
    p. cm. -- (Opposing viewpoints)
    Includes bibliographical references and index.
    ISBN 978-0-7377-4374-6 (hardcover)
    ISBN 978-0-7377-4373-9 (pbk.)
    1. Latin America--Juvenile literature. 2. Latin America--Economic conditions--Juvenile literature. 3. Latin America--Politics and government--Juvenile literature. 4. United States--Foreign relations--Latin America--Juvenile literature. 5. Latin America--Foreign relations--United States--Juvenile literature. 6. Human rights--Latin America--Juvenile literature. I. Gerdes, Louise I., 1953-
    F1408.2.L385 2009
    980--dc22
                                                      2009003287

Printed in the United States of America
1 2 3 4 5 6 7 13 12 11 10 09

JEFFERSON COUNTY PUBLIC LIBRARY
1143413612

Contents

Chapter 4: What Is the Status of Human Rights in Latin America?

Why Consider Opposing Viewpoints?

"The only way in which a human being can make some approach to knowing the whole of a subject is by hearing what can be said about it by persons of every variety of opinion and studying all modes in which it can be looked at by every character of mind. No wise man ever acquired his wisdom in any mode but this."

John Stuart Mill

In our media-intensive culture it is not difficult to find differing opinions. Thousands of newspapers and magazines and dozens of radio and television talk shows resound with differing points of view. The difficulty lies in deciding which opinion to agree with and which "experts" seem the most credible. The more inundated we become with differing opinions and claims, the more essential it is to hone critical reading and thinking skills to evaluate these ideas. Opposing Viewpoints books address this problem directly by presenting stimulating debates that can be used to enhance and teach these skills. The varied opinions contained in each book examine many different aspects of a single issue. While examining these conveniently edited opposing views, readers can develop critical thinking skills such as the ability to compare and contrast authors' credibility, facts, argumentation styles, use of persuasive techniques, and other stylistic tools. In short, the Opposing Viewpoints Series is an ideal way to attain the higher-level thinking and reading skills so essential in a culture of diverse and contradictory opinions.

In addition to providing a tool for critical thinking, Opposing Viewpoints books challenge readers to question their own strongly held opinions and assumptions. Most people form their opinions on the basis of upbringing, peer pressure, and personal, cultural, or professional bias. By reading carefully balanced opposing views, readers must directly confront new ideas as well as the opinions of those with whom they disagree. This is not to simplistically argue that everyone who reads opposing views will—or should—change his or her opinion. Instead, the series enhances readers' understanding of their own views by encouraging confrontation with opposing ideas. Careful examination of others' views can lead to the readers' understanding of the logical inconsistencies in their own opinions, perspective on why they hold an opinion, and the consideration of the possibility that their opinion requires further evaluation.

Evaluating Other Opinions

To ensure that this type of examination occurs, Opposing Viewpoints books present all types of opinions. Prominent spokespeople on different sides of each issue as well as well-known professionals from many disciplines challenge the reader. An additional goal of the series is to provide a forum for other, less known, or even unpopular viewpoints. The opinion of an ordinary person who has had to make the decision to cut off life support from a terminally ill relative, for example, may be just as valuable and provide just as much insight as a medical ethicist's professional opinion. The editors have two additional purposes in including these less known views. One, the editors encourage readers to respect others' opinions—even when not enhanced by professional credibility. It is only by reading or listening to and objectively evaluating others' ideas that one can determine whether they are worthy of consideration. Two, the inclusion of such viewpoints encourages the important critical thinking skill of objectively evaluating an author's credentials and bias. This evaluation will illuminate an author's reasons for taking a particular stance on an issue and will aid in readers' evaluation of the author's ideas.

It is our hope that these books will give readers a deeper understanding of the issues debated and an appreciation of the complexity of even seemingly simple issues when good and honest people disagree. This awareness is particularly important in a democratic society such as ours in which people enter into public debate to determine the common good. Those with whom one disagrees should not be regarded as enemies but rather as people whose views deserve careful examination and may shed light on one's own.

Thomas Jefferson once said that "difference of opinion leads to inquiry, and inquiry to truth." Jefferson, a broadly educated man, argued that "if a nation expects to be ignorant and free ... it expects what never was and never will be." As individuals and as a nation, it is imperative that we consider the opinions of others and examine them with skill and discernment. The Opposing Viewpoints Series is intended to help readers achieve this goal.

David L. Bender and Bruno Leone,
Founders

Introduction

> "The progress in democracy and human rights [in Latin America] has meant a difference in the lives of millions of people.... But the change is not irreversible, it can't be taken for granted and it hasn't gone as far as it needs to go."
>
> —William Spencer,
> Washington Office on Latin America

For some, Latin America evokes images of decorated military despots, camouflage-clad, cigar-smoking revolutionaries, frequent coups, corrupt governments, "disappeared" citizens, and murdered missionaries. Those who have visited or have close ties to the region know, however, that Latin America is an expansive region with a complex history, varied cultures, and vast natural and agricultural resources. Latin America encompasses Mexico, the nations of South and Central America, and the islands of the Caribbean. Indeed, one of the challenges of discussing Latin America justly is that the region includes many nations with different cultures, social structures, and economic and political histories.

When Europeans first came to Latin America, they found a variety of cultures, from the peaceful Guarani in the jungles of central South America to the sophisticated Inca, who with their formidable military carved out an empire that encompassed much of the Andes Mountains and the Pacific coast of South America. In the Caribbean, explorers encountered the Taino and other loosely organized hunter-gatherers, whom the conquerors quickly subjugated. In Mexico and Central America, explorers encountered the sophisticated Mayans and the aggressive Aztecs, who were organized and had a vast empire, like the Inca. While motives among the Spaniards and

Portuguese who came to Latin American during the late fifteenth and sixteenth centuries varied, conquest was the ultimate goal. Indeed, Spain and Portugal's colonial empire continued for three centuries and stretched from what is today California to the southernmost tip of South America, Cape Horn.

While the nations of Latin America are unique, they share this colonial past and the languages of their colonizers. In fact, this shared language is how Latin America is often defined. Another commonality among most Latin American nations is the social and economic stratification that has been a source of tension in the region for centuries. Commentators often consider the controversial region-wide gap between the rich and poor in debates over Latin America's economic challenges, political climate, foreign policy, and social conditions. While the region has shown significant political development over the years, centuries of revolutions and counter-revolutions have done little to bring about the social and economic changes that might reduce this enormous income gap. From the independence movement of the nineteenth century to the populist movement of the twenty-first century, Latin America remains a region that has more "have-nots," than "haves."

At the end of the eighteenth century, the new Latin American elites, the descendants of the early European settlers and the upper-class, mixed-race mestizos, sought independence from Spain and Portugal. Liberalized trade in the region had increased their prosperity and, in turn, their desire for autonomy. These often well-educated middle- and upper-class Latin Americans were inspired by revolutions in the United States and France. Thus, while Spain and Portugal were engulfed in the Napoleonic Wars that raged across Europe between 1803 and 1815, revolutionary leaders in Latin America began to declare independence and establish constitutional republics, cutting their colonial bonds. Unlike in France and the United States, however, no comparable social or economic

..volution accompanied independence in Latin America. No new classes came to power, and rule by the elite, which had characterized the colonial period, continued unchanged. Although the Latin American leaders who led the independence movement were inspired by revolutionary literature that gave primacy to the rights of the individual, once in power, they did nothing to address inequality or poverty.

The Latin American elite had little experience with governing—they had developed no political culture. The keys to good governance—the rule of law and the orderly transfer of political power—were rare among the new nations that emerged from the independence movement. In many nations, the early nineteenth century was typified by the rise of the *caudillo*, the strongman who came to power through the patronage of the elite or through force. These warlords exercised their power with little regard for law, and the rich grew richer while the peasants, who were forced to pay ever-increasing taxes, grew ever poorer. While powerful, these inexperienced leaders were poor stewards of the economy, and Latin America's economic situation spiraled downward. The Latin American political thinkers of the day began to look to the United States and Great Britain for strategies to reverse the region's economic downturn and at the same time address civil rights. Economic advancement, they observed, would increase political stability and promote freedom.

During the latter half of the nineteenth century, Latin America expanded the markets for its agricultural products and minerals. In some nations, leaders improved the country's infrastructure, which in turn facilitated commerce. New wealth and immigrants from Europe and Asia inspired efforts to modernize. Slavery was banned, universities were built, workers unionized, and some industries nationalized to protect workers. Increasingly, nations abandoned dictatorships to form republics. Nevertheless, many nations struggled to firmly establish democratic rule. In truth, with the exception of

Mexico and Costa Rica, every Latin American country had experienced at least one military coup during the twentieth century. Charismatic, authoritarian leaders would often take power, even in economically strong nations, such as Brazil and Argentina. In fact, the United States often contributed to democracy's failure in some countries by supporting dictators who opposed Communism and facilitated American imperialism in the region. Indeed, during the 1960s and early 1970s, the people of Brazil, Argentina, Chile, Uruguay, and Peru were under the thumb of brutal military dictatorships. Thus, despite some economic and democratic gains, early twentieth-century Latin America had yet to address the needs of its poorest citizens.

The political climate in Latin America again changed in the latter half of the twentieth century. Many corrupt leaders were driven from power in the 1980s, and after the fall of the Soviet Union, democracy and free markets began to thrive throughout the region. One nation after another held free and fair elections that led to peaceful changes of power. However, electoral democracy failed to achieve much in the way of civil rights and social justice. Since social gains were expected to accompany the spread of democracy and free markets, some analysts began to look outside Latin America for answers to the riddle of the region's persistent poverty and inequality. Some fault the market-oriented policies of multilateral lenders, such as the International Monetary Fund and the World Bank. Others point the finger at the U.S.-supported war on drugs. Still others continue to attribute the region's continuing economic and social stratification to inept leaders and poor governance.

The debate concerning how best to explain Latin America's failure to address economic and social inequality continues into the new millennium. In response to economic distress in the region, charismatic populist leaders are on the rise. Unlike their counterparts during the mid-twentieth century, however, the people have elected these leaders in free elections. Their rhetoric, however, remains the same, and the promise of economic security and equality is as yet unfulfilled. In Brazil, for example, 50 million people—almost a third of the population—live at or below the poverty line and 19 percent of all households still lack running water. The region's African descendent population makes up as much as half of its poor.

Some experts are therefore pessimistic about the region's future. In their view, Latin Americans are not yet politically mature enough to create prosperous, egalitarian societies. "They don't really have a vision for the future aside from each person's desire to increase their individual wealth," argues Heritage Foundation scholar Stephen Johnson. "Many people . . . don't understand that their personal prosperity is tied to that of their neighbors and of society as a whole, so they don't push hard enough for the kind of change they need, like strong legislatures and judiciaries and a government that actually listens to people." Other scholars are more optimistic. "I've met with a lot of the people who are in their 30s and 40s and are going to be running things soon, and I can tell you that these people are very impressive," says Georgetown University professor Michael Shifter. "They understand that governments have to be honest and effective and responsive," he maintains, "and that's what they're working for."

While the nations of Latin America strive to improve their position in the global political and economic landscape, commentators continue to debate the reasons for the region's challenges and how best to exploit its opportunities. The authors in *Opposing Viewpoints: Latin America* explore these and other issues in the following chapters: How Strong Are Latin American Economies? What Is the Political Climate in Latin America? What Role Should the United States Play in Latin America? and What Is the Status of Human Rights in Latin America? Colombian senator Gustavo Petro describes the period during the 1970s, when many Latin Americans tried to undertake peaceful change, as a Latin American spring. Tragically, he claims, tens of thousands were hunted down and killed. Petro has renewed hope, however, stating, "Societies [in Latin America] will be able to take up the issue of social inequality, and to deepen democracy." For many Latin Americans, Petro predicts, "Another spring is here."

CHAPTER 1

How Strong Are Latin American Economies?

Chapter Preface

Latin American economies, like the troubled world economy, have been in a slump since the beginning of the new millennium. Indeed, the growth Latin America experienced between 1960 and 1980 has declined significantly. There have been signs of improvement in recent years: Brazil, Argentina, and Venezuela, for example, have financial reserves to reduce dependence on other nations for capital. Decreasing poverty in several Latin American nations has expanded internal markets, which puts these nations in a better position to survive the global economic turbulence. Generally, however, the region's economic success has faltered, and commentators continue to contest what policies have led to its economic decline. One of several debates concerning the strength of Latin American economies is the role the International Monetary Fund (IMF) played in the region's current economic crisis.

Some analysts argue that IMF policies played a significant role in Latin America's economic decline. The IMF, an organization in which the United States has a great deal of influence, lends tens of billions of dollars each year to Latin American nations. This provides the IMF with significant influence over the economic policies of these countries. According to IMF opponents, the IMF forced Latin American nations to adopt steps for economic reform that have proven disastrous. These neoliberal economic policies, often referred to as the Washington Consensus, removed trade barriers, privatized state-owned industries, and opened markets to foreign capital. This one-size-fits-all policy, IMF opponents assert, did not take into account the economic situations of individual Latin American countries. According to economic scholar Mark Weisbrot, "Basically, there has been this experiment where they've forced these countries to implement tight fiscal policies and open trade and monetary polices regardless of what was happening on the ground, and it has failed." While these policies may have jump-started the economies of some Latin American nations, IMF opponents maintain, they have been disastrous in others.

IMF officials dispute these claims. "One-size-fits-all is a big myth," asserts Tom Dawson, the IMF's chief spokesperson. "We're always accused of not caring what [client countries] think, but we look closely at every individual country and try to help them fashion policies to suit their needs." Dawson cites, for example, IMF policies in Argentina. "The Washington Consensus calls for flexible currency-exchange rates, and yet when Argentina told the fund that they were going to have a fixed rate, we accepted it as the right policy." IMF supporters also cite cases in which the Washington Consensus has led to positive economic outcomes. IMF loans and advice have improved the economic situation in Chile, "and they've paid off their IMF loans ahead of schedule," Dawson notes. IMF supporters argue instead that the economic problems of Latin American nations are largely of their own making. According to foreign policy scholar Julia E. Sweig, "They're not doing the things good governments should do to make their economies grow." Those who support Washington Consensus policies argue that many Latin American governments waste money or spend beyond their means. "Blaming the fund for the reality that every country must confront its budget constraints is like blaming the fund for gravity," claims IMF research director Kenneth Rogoff.

As the United States and other nations continue to court influence in Latin America, commentators will contest whether the economic challenges of Latin America's nations are of their own making or the result of economic policies some argue were forced upon them by the IMF. The authors in the following chapter debate this and other issues concerning the strength of Latin American economies.

> *"In many ways, the past half-decade has been a remarkably encouraging period for Latin America, both politically and economically."*

Latin American Economies Are Improving

Duncan Currie

In the following viewpoint, Duncan Currie maintains that despite gloomy reports in the media, Latin America is showing signs of economic improvement. For example, he asserts, the region has averaged 5.5 percent growth in gross domestic product. Moreover, some populist policy reforms promote anti-inflationary measures and debt reduction, Currie claims. Those Latin America nations that export natural resources and encourage foreign investment have seen historic economic growth, he reasons. Currie is the managing editor of The American, *a libertarian magazine.*

As you read, consider the following questions:

1. What gains has the center-right government of Álvaro Uribe made in Colombia, in Currie's opinion?

Duncan Currie, "The Good News from Latin America," *The American,* November 15, 2007. Reproduced with the permission of the American Enterprise Institute for Public Policy Research, Washington, D.C.

2. What impact has President Luiz Inácio Lula da Silva had in Brazil, according to the author?

3. In the author's opinion, why is it important to distinguish the market-friendly democratic left from the anti-market radical left?

There is no shortage of bad news from Latin America. Drug violence is escalating in Mexico. The . . . Guatemalan presidential campaign was marred by bloodshed. The new leader of Panama's national assembly is a pro-Noriega radical who has been indicted in U.S. court for the 1992 murder of an American soldier. Buoyed by high oil prices, anti-American populist Hugo Chávez continues to pursue a failed economic model and unravel Venezuelan democracy. He now has acolytes in Bolivia and Ecuador, plus a budding alliance with Nicaraguan President Daniel Ortega and chummy relations with Argentina. Newspapers describe a "leftist" surge that is supposedly sweeping the region—a region wracked by corruption, poverty, inequality, an education gap, and rampant crime. According to the World Bank, Latin America remains one of the most difficult places on Earth to do business; it ranks "at the bottom of the list of reformers" worldwide. For that matter, as the International Monetary Fund notes in its latest World Economic Outlook, "the region continues to be at the bottom of the world growth league."

A Need for Perspective

Yet amid all the doom and gloom, some perspective is needed. In many ways, the past half-decade has been a remarkably encouraging period for Latin America, both politically and economically. Most governments have upheld the institutions of democracy and embraced responsible fiscal policies. "Economic management has really never been better," says Peter Hakim, president of the Inter-American Dialogue. "Democratic politics is really very healthy in Latin America. This is a good period for the region."

Indeed, there is "definitely a lot of reason to be optimistic," says Alberto Ramos, senior Latin America economist at Goldman Sachs. In 2002, the region was just beginning to recover from a series of economic crises. Today, "It's a completely different reality," says Ramos. "The overall policy mix is definitely much stronger."

As Diana Farrell and Susan Lund of the McKinsey Global Institute observe in the latest *Milken Institute Review*, "Real GDP [gross domestic product] growth has averaged 5.5 percent over the last three years, compared with just 2.1 percent in 1995 to 2002. Gross domestic savings are up as well, to 21.7 percent in 2002 to 2005 from 19.8 percent in 1995 to 2002."

True, Latin America still suffers from a dearth of financial assets. But even here, the situation has improved. "Since 2002," write Farrell and Lund, "the region's stock of financial assets has grown at 18 percent annually (adjusted for exchange rate changes), up from just 5 percent in 1995 to 2002." Between 2002 and 2006, it jumped from $1.7 trillion to over $4 trillion. "Equity market capitalization has increased even more," note Farrell and Lund, "and the region's markets have outperformed emerging markets as a whole by 40 percent."

The Top Economic Reformers

Ramos believes some of the most important policy reforms included anti-inflationary measures, steps to promote central bank independence, and deficit and debt reduction. He lauds Chile's "impeccable" fiscal policies, and lists Colombia, Brazil, Peru, and Mexico among the region's other top economic reformers.

In Colombia, the center-right government of Álvaro Uribe has achieved historic security gains since 2002 and created the conditions for rapid economic growth. Murders, kidnappings, and terrorist attacks are all way down. The left-wing guerrillas have been driven into the jungles and thousands of the right-wing paramilitaries have been demobilized. [In 2006]

Colombia's GDP grew at its fastest pace (6.8 percent) since the late 1970s. *Business Week* now touts Colombia as an "investment hot spot."

In Brazil, President Luiz Inácio Lula da Silva has curbed inflation and slashed poverty through pragmatic, market-oriented policies. Despite his past history as a left-wing union leader, he has governed from the moderate center-left, in stark contrast to Chávez. Brazil is now experiencing low-inflation growth, which is slowly chipping away at inequality. "Recent data from the Brazilian National Statistics Institute (IBGE) brings encouraging news," the BBC reported in September, "with average incomes rising by 7.2 percent in 2006. The increase was biggest among the less well off, and in the northeast." In recent years, millions of Brazilians have entered the middle class, a trend that has also been visible in Mexico.

An Historic Economic Expansion

"Latin America's present expansion is its longest since the 1960s, and sustained growth has helped reduce external vulnerabilities," says the IMF's [International Monetary Fund] World Economic Outlook. "Latin American economies have allowed exchange rates to move more flexibly than in the past," and have also "liberalized restrictions on capital outflows." Meanwhile, the spike in global commodity prices has provided a boon to those countries rich in minerals.

"In some ways, Latin America has never had it better," former Clinton administration official Eric Farnsworth said in a speech [in October 2007]. "Economic growth across the region is at historic highs, particularly in nations that export natural resources and primary products in agriculture, energy, and mining. Even the so-called populists speak in the language of fiscal restraint, low inflation, and attracting foreign investment," said Farnsworth, who now serves as vice president of the Council of the Americas. "Democracy across the region requires nurturing but it is largely secure, and human rights have never been more respected."

What about the blustery Chávez? Isn't he attracting broad Latin American support? In fact, the Venezuelan gadfly has high negatives throughout the region. Of the seven Latin American nations polled in the 2007 Pew Global Attitudes Survey, majorities in Chile (75 percent), Brazil (74 percent), Peru (70 percent), Mexico (66 percent), and Bolivia (59 percent) expressed little or no confidence in Chávez "to do the right thing regarding world affairs." Even in Argentina, perhaps the most anti-American country in the region, 43 percent of respondents had little or no confidence in Chávez.

In the same poll, majorities in Venezuela (72 percent), Brazil (65 percent), Chile (60 percent), Mexico (55 percent), and Bolivia (53 percent), along with a plurality in Peru (47 percent), agreed that "most people are better off in a free-market economy, even though some people are rich and some are poor." As Pew reported, "There is broad support for free-market economic policies across Latin America, despite the election in the past decade of leftist leaders." Indeed, majorities in Venezuela (74 percent), Brazil (70 percent), Mexico (65 percent), Chile (63 percent), and Peru (61 percent), along with a plurality in Bolivia (49 percent), said that foreign companies were having a "good" impact on their countries.

Distinguishing the Leftist Movements

In terms of the "leftist" electoral wave, it is crucially important to distinguish the market-friendly democratic left from the anti-market radical left. As foreign policy scholar Walter Russell Mead has written in *The New Republic*, "Latin America is now beginning to acquire something it has sorely lacked: a left-of-center political leadership able to combine its mission of serving the poor with a firm commitment to currency stability, the rule of law, and the development of a favorable business climate."

A Reason for Hope

Latin America is doing better than at any time since the 1960s. Economic growth has averaged over 5% a year since 2004, inflation has been generally low, direct investment is arriving in record quantities, and the region's current account and fiscal accounts are both in surplus. Of course the average conceals wide (and widening) variations. But to the surprise of some, the credit crunch has so far had little discernible effect. Indeed, as world prices for many of Latin America's key commodity exports continue to rise, the pace of growth has even accelerated in some countries.

"A Coming Test of Virtue; Latin America's Economies,"
The Economist, *April 12, 2008.*

This has been amply demonstrated by the current center-left governments of Chile, Brazil, Peru, and Uruguay, which rank among the most pro-market regimes in the region. The leaders of these countries have become models for other left-wing politicians. After Álvaro Colom won this month's Guatemalan presidential election, Reuters reported that "Colom defines himself as a moderate social democrat and says he is inspired by leftist presidents Luiz Inácio Lula da Silva in Brazil and Michelle Bachelet in Chile. He says his government would not clash with the landowning and business elites of Guatemala, a major coffee producer."

There is no question that Latin populism has reemerged, with the aid of Venezuelan petrodollars. And if Ecuador, Bolivia, and Nicaragua follow the Chávez route, that will be bad news for their citizens. But these are three of the weakest, poorest countries in the region, without much influence or strategic value. For that matter, it's not as if free markets have failed in Venezuela, Ecuador, Bolivia, and Nicaragua. The much-maligned "Washington consensus" (or "neoliberal") reforms were never really applied there, due to massive corruption.

A Need for Reform

Latin America remains beset by staggering socioeconomic difficulties, which is why the siren song of populism can be so alluring. "It's still the slowest growing region in the world, and that is a concern," says Ramos. Moving forward, Farrell and Lund argue for reinforcing central bank independence (following the lead of Chile and Mexico), trimming inflation, and eliminating budget deficits. In the legal realm, they note that Latin America needs much better contract enforcement and investor protection, not to mention sweeping bankruptcy and judicial reforms.

U.S. policy is at a crossroads. Democrats routinely criticize [U.S. President] George Bush for "alienating" allies around the world. But if the Democratic Congress kills a bilateral free trade pact with Colombia[1] it will severely damage America's image in Latin America and deal a blow to regional cooperation. If such cooperation unravels, Chávez is ready to fill the vacuum. So are the resource-hungry Chinese.

As Farnsworth has put it, "The United States must choose, whether or not to prioritize the Americas, helping the people of the region attain their highest aspirations, supporting reformers who are politically exposed and taking a chance by working closely with the United States, while pursuing shared values and common interests with regional allies and friends. Otherwise, if we delay or choose not to decide, the choice will be made for us."

---

1. As of September 2008, the United States failed to ratify a free trade agreement with Colombia.

"Each [Latin American] country's choices are dependent more on its own dynamics that defy labels rather than on some supposed continental wave."

The Success of Latin American Economies Vary from Nation to Nation

Ken Frankel

In the following viewpoint, Ken Frankel argues that Latin American economic policies depend on each nation's distinct economic, social, and cultural circumstances, not media-assigned political labels. For example, the market-based policies of Chile's Michelle Bachelet would not work in Luiz Inácio Lula da Silva's Brazil, which has a significant internal market and diverse foreign trade, Frankel maintains. One unifying factor, he asserts, is a general discontent with the U.S.-promoted economic policies of the 1980s and 1990s, which failed to alleviate widespread poverty. Frankel is a lawyer and director of the Canadian Foundation for the Americas.

Ken Frankel, "Forget About Right, Left—It's Latin America," *Globe & Mail* (Toronto, Canada), December 12, 2006, p. A23. Copyright © 2006 Bell Globemedia Interactive. Reproduced by permission of the author.

As you read, consider the following questions:

1. According to Frankel, what do Latin Americans know will happen in China, India, and other Asian countries as Latin America's economies inch along?

2. What makes the United States an easy target for Latin American politicians hoping to carve out a niche for themselves, in the author's view?

3. What does the author claim is a "witch's brew" in each Latin American country?

The so-called leftist tsunami sweeping through Latin America should be downgraded to a tropical storm.

[During 2006], Latin America has completed a cycle of 12 elections. In its wake, breathless press reports decry a hard leftist tide (with revolutionary undertones) washing over the hemisphere, and pundits are trying to distinguish among "responsible leftists," leftist demagogues and populists. Though the explanations are an admirable attempt to explain why certain economic and political choices are being taken, none is satisfying. Latin America's political and economic choices have once again shown that the hemisphere does not wear well the imported "right" and "left" labels. Each country's choices are dependent more on its own dynamics that defy labels rather than on some supposed continental wave.

A Generalized Discontent

There is unquestionably a generalized discontent, and rightly so, about the persistence of massive poverty and the world's largest chasm between the haves and have-nots. Much of the discontent has focused on the disappointing results in most countries (though with encouraging signs in the past couple of years) of the so-called neo-liberal economic principles embraced since the mid-1980s. Known as the "Washington consensus," it has been viewed as a tool of First World (primarily U.S.) big capital, in cahoots with the World Bank, the International Monetary Fund and Latin elites.

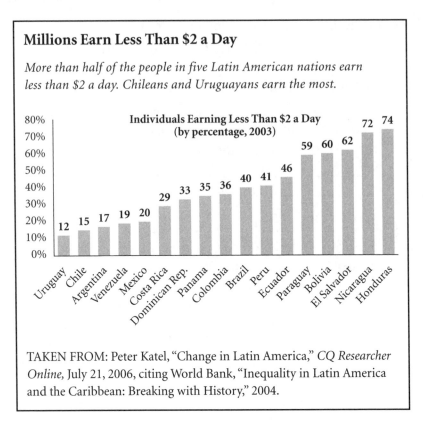

Millions Earn Less Than $2 a Day

More than half of the people in five Latin American nations earn less than $2 a day. Chileans and Uruguayans earn the most.

Individuals Earning Less Than $2 a Day (by percentage, 2003)

TAKEN FROM: Peter Katel, "Change in Latin America," *CQ Researcher Online,* July 21, 2006, citing World Bank, "Inequality in Latin America and the Caribbean: Breaking with History," 2004.

Latin Americans know that, as their economies inch along, China, India and other Asian countries are outstripping them in the global production chain.

The model was underthought, oversold and, in several cases, corruptly executed. But, with the possible exception of tax and spending policies, there is very little inherently "rightist" about the Washington consensus or inherently "leftist" about its predecessor model.

But the perception is that, by backing the model, as the "Washington" moniker indicates, the U.S. is culpable for its failures. The disappointing results, along with the generalized disdain for President George [W.] Bush in the hemisphere, make the U.S. an easy target for politicians seeking to carve out a niche for themselves by promising a new economic path.

No One Model

Despite the histrionics, political pandering and otherwise silly rhetoric of some (such as Venezuela's Hugo Chavez), however, it would be a mistake to assume that those leaders who pledge to rework the economic model represent a radical shift from new thinking among developmental economists. Such economists agree that increasing investment and productivity are the sine qua non [essential] for development and that programs targeting education, sanitation and health care are critical to development. They also seem to agree that there is no one model that can be applied for all of the countries, all of whom have distinct economic, social, cultural and political circumstances.

But that's where the agreement seems to end. And that's where developmental economics becomes one part social science and one part alchemy. How and where to use state intervention and fiscal, trade and monetary policies is a witch's brew in each country. Some markets work better than others. A lot of what has worked in Chile, which has had the most success in combining the Washington consensus model with other programs, won't necessarily work in Brazil, with its large internal market, diversified foreign trade and its own social and political characteristics.

Nor would it work in the mineral-based economies of Venezuela, Bolivia or Ecuador. It's not a question of "right" or "left" economics but rather of economic development to solve the sluggish growth and lopsided distribution of wealth. Even the latest alleged poster boy for economic adventurism in Latin America, Bolivian President Evo Morales, has not ventured far from the menu of economic measures being considered by developmental economists.

His "nationalization" of foreign-owned gas assets turned out to be little more than a raise in royalty rights to levels seen in most other gas regions of the world. (By comparison,

Russia's [former president] Vladimir Putin has undertaken a much more far-reaching nationalization program, and by more underhanded means.)

A Mix of Mechanisms

What's also particularly interesting about the recent cycle of elections is how much the economic options of the "leftist" winners, such as Brazil's Luiz Inacio Lula da Silva and Chile's Michelle Bachelet, may resemble those of newly installed "rightist" Mexican President Felipe Calderon. The nearing convergence, at least among three of the region's advanced economies, is not coincidental. Each uses a mix of market mechanisms and state-sponsored programs. The circumstances in each country will dictate what is workable.

Our concern should not be what Venezuela's President has done thus far but rather what he hasn't and likely won't do. He has raised hopes in many around the hemisphere by promising a successful alternative to the current economic structure. While his literacy and education programs are a step forward, he has introduced few innovations in his eight years in office to deal with Venezuela's fundamental economic problems. If he doesn't succeed despite having an ocean of oil and strong internal political support at his disposal, then where will his disillusioned followers turn?

Then we may see what a tsunami looks like.

> *"The people of the Americas understand the relationship between their subordination and the penetration of their local and national governments by the neoliberal imperative."*

U.S. Foreign Policies Failed to Improve Latin American Economies

Christy Thornton

In the following viewpoint, Christy Thornton claims that U.S. neoliberal economic policies—deregulating markets, liberalizing trade and finance, and privatizing public business—failed to achieve the promised economic growth in Latin America. Indeed, she asserts, Latin American impatience with these failed policies has led to uprisings, protests, and the democratic election of leaders who promise to free Latin Americans from the yoke of U.S. imperialism. Thornton is director of the North American Congress on Latin America (NACLA), which works to free Latin America and the Caribbean from oppression and injustice.

Christy Thornton, "Back on the Map," *NACLA Report on the Americas*, vol. 40, January/February 2007, pp. 3–4. Copyright © 2007 by the North American Congress on Latin America, 38 Greene St. 4th FL., New York, NY 10013. Reproduced by permission.

As you read, consider the following questions:

1. In Thornton's opinion, how has *Foreign Policy* editor Moisés Naím failed to assess anti-American impatience in Latin America?

2. How should people see 2006, the "year of elections" in Latin America, in the author's view?

3. According to the author, what has been NACLA's impact over the years?

In a recent piece in *Foreign Policy* magazine, editor Moisés Naím argued that Latin America has become a "lost continent," and that the region "can't compete on the world stage—not even as a threat." Even the anti-Americanism emanating from our south, most readily embodied in Venezuela's Hugo Chávez, doesn't hold the weight of the growing legions of suicide bombers of Iraq, Afghanistan and their neighbors. While recognizing that leftist leaders elected [since 2001] are far from monolithic, Naím argues that "prolonged mediocre economic performance" is a cornerstone of the dissatisfaction sweeping the region, and that it unites the people of Latin America in their sense of "rage, revenge, and impatience" with their political leaders. Patience, he argues, is needed to solve the problems of Latin America and reverse the decades of poor economic performance. Patience, he says, will put the region "back on the map."

A History of Economic Subjugation

Perhaps it should not be surprising that a technocrat such as Naím would fail to connect the anti-Americanist impatience he ascribes to some 500 million people with the decades-long history of economic subjugation to the hegemonic doctrines promoted by the United States and the international financial institutions; it is far easier to ignore history than engage it. "Latin Americans," he reminds us, "have been experimenting with brutal, heavy handed swings in their political economy

Neoliberalism: A Failed Model

The neoliberal model failed to consolidate the social forces necessary for its stabilization, resulting in the early onset of crises that would check its course. The three largest Latin American economies were the theatre for the most dramatic crises: Mexico in 1994, Brazil in 1999 and Argentina in 2002; the programme crumbled without delivering on its promises. The ravages of hyper-inflation were checked, but this was only achieved at tremendous cost. For a decade or more, economic development was paralysed, the concentration of wealth grew greater than ever before, public deficits spiralled and the mass of the population had their rights expropriated, most notably in the domain of employment and labour relations. On top of this, national debt expanded exponentially and regional economies became highly vulnerable, helplessly exposed to attack from speculators, as these three countries each discovered to their cost.

Emir Sader, "The Weakest Link? Neoliberalism in Latin America," New Left Review, *July/August 2008. www.newleftreview.org.*

since the 1970s." We can only assume that the brutal heavy-handedness to which Naím refers, though he makes no mention of it, is the steady entrenchment of U.S.-promoted neoliberalism first introduced in Chile in the early 1980s and then sown throughout the region under the auspices of structural adjustment and, later, the Washington Consensus. [Neoliberalism, also known as the Washington Consensus, requires deregulating markets, liberalizing trade and finance, and privatizing public business.] To be sure, it was Latin American elites who put these policies into place, but, as Paul Drake argues in a new NACLA [North American Congress on Latin America] book, "the celerity with which most of the Latin American republics capitulated to [the neoliberal] U.S. offensive in the 1980s and 1990s was stunning." Latin America was to be the proving ground for the neoliberal project, which was to stabilize the region after the debt crisis, jumpstart economic growth, and make the region competitive on the world stage. State-owned enterprises and services were privatized, social institutions and protections were eroded, wages and per capita income stagnated—and, as we all know, the growth never materialized. The showpieces of the doctrine—first Mexico, then Argentina—suffered near total collapse. And yet, Naím would have us believe that Latin America's impatience with this legacy will be the region's undoing, and that only a moderation beholden to the imperative of economic stability will lift Latin America's 165 million impoverished people from their squalor and put them "back on the map."

Meanwhile, the people of Latin America aren't waiting to be put back on someone else's map. Demonstrations, uprisings, and elections from Chile to Los Angeles have made clear that the peoples of the Americas are no longer content to wait and see who might finally deliver on the promises made over the past 40 years. Perhaps the most striking feature of this "impatience" is the structural analysis put forth by everyday people throughout the hemisphere. From students in Chile to miners in Bolivia, from teachers in Oaxaca [Mexico] to restaurant workers in Chicago, the people of the Americas understand the relationship between their subordination and the penetration of their local and national governments by the neoliberal imperative.

The Beginning of a New Era

To be sure, this frustration with the legitimacy of local and national governments is having repercussions for governability, as we are seeing so vividly in Oaxaca. But in a region where the needs of the people have been so long subordinated to the imperative of economic growth and stability (even as that growth and stability have failed to materialize), new models of and for inclusion must be built into Latin America's democratic processes. In this way, 2006, as the "year of elections," should be seen not as the end of the neoliberal period—indeed, this moment is a highly uncertain one and the interests behind the neoliberal imperative remain firmly entrenched—but as the beginning of a new era, in which Latin America rebuilds its social democratic traditions, breaks free of the constraints of imperialism, and reorients the very map from which it has been so easily erased.

How fitting, then, that the birth of this new era should coincide with NACLA entering its fifth decade. We celebrate in 2007 the 40th anniversary of the publication of the first *NACLA Newsletter*, a mimeographed eight pages that signaled the arrival of what would become the most-widely read English-language publication on Latin America. NACLA's achievements over the last few decades, chronicled by Fred Rosen on the occasion of our 35th anniversary and published in the *Report*, mirrored the ever-changing political situation in Latin America. During dark periods of dictatorship and civil war, the *NACLA Report* brought readers in the U.S. information they could not find anywhere else, and directly challenged structures of power throughout the Americas. NACLA changed the lives of scholar activists in the Chile and Central America solidarity movements, and as our FBI file shows, was a force to be reckoned with.

Of course, our anniversary provided an opportunity to reflect not only on what we've done, but on what role we play now. Clearly, a great deal has changed since 1967. Though our mission—to provide information and analysis as tools for education and advocacy—remains as relevant as ever, the way people search for and use information has changed dramatically, even in the last decade. So we had to think carefully

about how people use NACLA and the information we provide, and how best to reach new people who are seeking to
make sense of the world in order to change it. In this process,
it became clear that we had been assuming that our long and
prestigious history was enough to see us through and ensure
our longevity. I was, therefore, charged with the somewhat
daunting task of moving an organization as venerable as NA-
CLA forward, into a new era in which we would be not only
what we once were, but *more*: reach more people, provide
more information and, above all, make more of an impact.

"There is little reason for progressives to be optimistic about the economic policy direction of Latin America's new leaders."

Populist Policies Will Not Improve Latin American Economies

Matías Vernengo

In the following viewpoint, Matías Vernengo asserts that the resurgence of leftist leaders in Latin America may appear to be a sign of dramatic change but, in reality, the economic policies of these left-leaning leaders are little different from previous regimes. In fact, Vernengo maintains, efforts to make fiscal discipline a priority have prevented spending on promised social programs and have done little to reduce unemployment or poverty. Any growth, Vernengo claims, is a result of increased trade rather than innovative economic policies. Vernengo is a professor of economics at the University of Utah.

Matías Vernengo, "Latin America's Left Off Track: Latin America Has a New Crop of Leftist Leaders, but Their Macroeconomic Policies Are Sadly Familiar," *Dollars & Sense*, vol. 259, May/June 2005, pp. 21–24. Copyright © 2005 Economic Affairs Bureau, Inc. Reproduced by permission of *Dollars & Sense*, a progressive economics magazine. www .dollarsandsense.org.

41

As you read, consider the following questions:

1. To what do observers of the region usually credit Latin America's turn to leftist politics, in Vernengo's view?
2. What Keynesian fiscal policies are considered the hallmarks of a progressive government, in the author's opinion?
3. According to the author, what has been the result of efforts to contain deficits and reduce the burden of debt in Latin America?

For several years, electoral results in Latin America have been shifting leftward. The victory of Tabaré Vázquez in Uruguay is [an] example; the list also includes Néstor Kirchner in Argentina, Luis Inácio Lula da Silva in Brazil, Ricardo Lagos in Chile, Lucio Gutiérrez in Ecuador, and Hugo Chávez in Venezuela. The new left governments are a mix in their political provenance. Lagos is from the well-established Socialist Party, while Lula and Vázquez represent newer parties gaining power for the first time. Kirchner, from the Partido Justicialista (Peronists), Chávez, and Gutiérrez are more typical of the old Latin American populism in which personalities are more important than political parties.

Beyond these center-left electoral victories, it is clear that the majority of civil society in Latin America rejects the neoliberal policies imposed during the 1990s. Popular demonstrations against privatization and trade liberalization are widespread. October [2004] saw a dramatic revolt in Bolivia, for example, where a coalition of labor unions and indigenous peoples, spurred by the government's plan to privatize the nation's gas reserves, brought about the resignation of President Sanchez de Lozada and strengthened the position of the indigenous leader Evo Morales.

A Momentous Step

The resurgence of the left is a momentous step in Latin America. The election of Ricardo Lagos, Chile's first Socialist president since the 1973 military coup against Salvador Allende, is a landmark, as are the victories in Brazil and Uruguay of new-style left governments embedded in deep-seated social movements. The political changes underway in Latin America today are comparable to the victories of Felipe Gonzalez after the long night of [Francisco] Franco's dictatorship in Spain [1936–75], and the ... revival of the Labor Party under Tony Blair following Margaret Thatcher's conservative reign [in Great Britain]. These victories are significant, especially because they reflect the region's long process of redemocratization, a political shift which has gone hand in hand with the revival of civic life: the rise of empowered indigenous movements, renewed struggles for land reform, worker occupations of factories to keep them operating in the face of economic collapse, the rise of *asambleas* (neighborhood assemblies) meeting to discuss the way forward for antineoliberalism protests.

Observers of the region have usually credited this left turn to dissatisfaction with the neoliberal, "Washington Consensus" policies imposed during the 1990s. The Washington Consensus basically required deregulating markets, liberalizing trade and finance, and privatizing public firms. The emphasis was on price stabilization, fiscal austerity, and market-friendly policies, a mix that ultimately favored international financial markets and the local elites who could benefit from a more open financial environment. Arguably, if the left is to stake out a new direction and change the region for the better, economic policies will have to be at the center of the social transformation. Notwithstanding the political importance of Latin America's recent left turn, however, there is little reason for progressives to be optimistic about the economic policy direction of Latin America's new leaders. . . .

Good Luck, Not Good Policies

If Keynesian fiscal policies—progressive taxation, increased spending on social programs, and deficit spending to maintain full employment—are the hallmarks of a progressive government, then the new left governments in Latin America cannot be seen as particularly progressive.

Despite variations in political discourse, the countries' macroeconomic policies are broadly similar, and represent little change from those of the previous regimes. The continuity of macroeconomic policies is most evident in the arena of fiscal policy. All the center-left governments in the region have accepted the logic behind an emphasis on fiscal discipline: that high fiscal deficits cause inflation, and, by generating fears of default, cause capital flight and lead to balance-of-payments problems. All accept the dictum that they cannot pursue more progressive fiscal policies because international financial markets would punish their countries with a run on their currencies.

All of these center-left governments are prioritizing fiscal austerity to control government debt accumulation and are committed to maintaining primary surpluses even in periods of recession. (Primary surpluses correspond to the difference between spending and revenues, but excluding interest payments on outstanding debt. In other words, a government with revenues of $100 that pays $35 in interest payments and $70 on other expenditures would have a nominal deficit of $5 but a primary surplus of $30.) This is a significant change compared to the Keynesian approaches that dominated policymaking in the region prior to the 1990s and is more extreme than the anti-Keynesian bias in the developed world. The consequences are stark: maintaining primary fiscal surpluses has squeezed public investment and spending on social programs, dampened economic growth, and favored financial interests and the well-to-do.

The Impact of External Factors

Although exchange-rate policies vary somewhat, most Latin American governments across the political spectrum today emphasize the role of exchange rates in controlling inflation. Their role in promoting external competitiveness has become secondary. By controlling exchange rates, governments are able to keep the prices of imported goods, which crucially affect inflation, down. But this also means that the prices of domestic products are less competitive, and so hobbles the development of domestic industries.

At times exchange rate controls are seen as a temporary device to avoid balance-of-payments crises, but not as instrumental in promoting development. For example, Argentina adopted capital controls after the December 2000 crisis, but these are intended to be temporary. None of the left governments has made capital controls (such as foreign exchange controls or Tobin taxes [a tax on the trade of currency across borders]) central to its economic agenda. Capital controls reduce the outflows and inflows of foreign currencies. With capital controls in place, the rate of interest does not need to be hiked to avoid capital outflows and can be adjusted for domestic purposes. Hence, capital controls put national governments in control of monetary policy.

If the macroeconomic policies of the region's left regimes are successful, perhaps it doesn't matter whether or not they are progressive. In fact, ... economic performance in Latin America has been exceptional. According to the Economic Commission for Latin America and the Caribbean (ECLAC), the economies of the region exceeded expectations in 2004, with an average regional GDP [gross domestic product] growth rate of 5.5%, surpassing the world average rate of 4%. Venezuela grew by an incredible 18%, Argentina by around 8%, and Chile and Brazil by slightly above 5%.

However, these strong growth rates have more to do with external drivers than with any innovative policies of the region's new leaders. Ultimately, the remarkable expansion of China, which has increased its trade with Latin America considerably, the United States' mild recovery, and an improvement in the terms of trade—the relative price of Latin America's exports—explain the positive Latin American performance. That external factors are propelling the region's economies casts serious doubt on the sustainability of their growth. The economic policies pursued by the left will not be of much help if economic growth in China and the United States slows down in the near future, as many analysts expect. Good luck more than good policies is behind the new prosperity.

The Consequences of Current Fiscal Policies

Economic growth alone is not enough to improve the lot of the region's poor anyway. Brazil's story illustrates the distributive consequences of the current fiscal policies in the region, and highlights the continuity with the policies of past administrations. [In 2004] Lula signed his second agreement with the International Monetary Fund (IMF). The agreement, which requires Brazil to adopt the usual litany of neoliberal policies, particularly cutting government spending, was all but necessary, and Lula decided to sign it only to gain credibility with international financial markets.

In Brazil's case, the primary surpluses (4.25% of GDP in 2003) go hand in hand with large nominal deficits (5% of GDP in 2003). The difference between a primary surplus and a nominal deficit represents interest payments made to the owners of government bonds. That is, almost 10% of Brazil's GDP was transferred [in 2004] to bond holders, mostly corporations and wealthy individuals. Interest payments represent almost half of Brazilian government expenditures, and are considerably higher than the amounts spent on Zero Hunger, land reform, or First Job, to name a few of the well-publicized social programs of Lula's Workers' Party. The result is that the income distribution in Brazil, one of the world's most unequal countries, is no better now than when Lula took office in 2003, and probably slightly worse. The share of wages in total income in Brazil fell from 36.1% in 2002 to 35.6% in 2003.

Constraints in Argentina

Argentina and Venezuela face similar constraints, but because of more closed capital accounts and lower rates of interest their plight is less extreme. In Argentina, Kirchner is negotiating fiercely with the IMF and the private creditors who allowed the country to obtain a favorable rescheduling of foreign debt. Yet [in 2004] his government maintained a primary surplus even greater than the 3% of GDP its prior agreement with the IMF called for. The IMF has let it be known that future approvals of the debt-restructuring program, and hence additional money, will be forthcoming only if Kirchner maintains fiscal austerity.

More important, Argentina has tentatively agreed to gradually scrap all the capital controls implemented since its currency crisis in 2001. Argentina's interest rates today are considerably lower than Brazil's, and close to the U.S. real rate of interest. (Brazil does not impose controls on capital flows.) If Argentina complies, the country can expect higher interest rates in the near future.

Kirchner has been accused of promoting irresponsible economic policies and favoring unsustainable redistribution towards the poor, but it's hard to see why. Argentina's current fiscal stance will require continued primary surpluses to pay for debt servicing. It's true that the government established a program of transfers to the unemployed (Plan Jefes de Hogar), but the benefits are insufficient, and other public investments are simply not being made. Maintaining primary surpluses means that the resources available for social transfers, including the Plan Jefes de Hogar, are severely constrained. Overall, then, with the exception of the fixed exchange-rate system, Kirchner's government is adhering to basically the same set of macroeconomic policies that prevailed through the 1990s.

Latin America's Left Leaders

ARGENTINA
Nester Kirchner, Justicialist
Party, 2003

BRAZIL
Luís Inacio Lula da silva,
Workers party, 2003

CHILE
Ricardo Lagos Socialist Party,
2000

ECUADOR
Lucin Gutierrez, no party, 2003
[deposed April 2005]

URUGUAY
Tabare Vazquez, Broad Front,
2005

VENEZUELA
Hugo Chavez, Movement for
the Fifth Republic, 1999

TAKEN FROM: Matías Vernengo, "Latin America's Left off Track,"
Dollars & Sense, May/June 2005.

The Venezuelan Story

The Venezuelan story is similar. Chávez's 1998 government program (La Propuesta de Hugo Chávez para Transformar Venezuela) designated inflation as the country's central macroeconomic problem. Since then, an overvalued exchange rate has been his administration's main instrument for reducing the price of imported goods and keeping inflation in check. Lula also uses a managed and appreciated exchange rate to control inflation, as did his predecessor Fernando Henrique Cardoso; Argentina, under the 1991 Convertibility Plan, which pegged the country's currency to the dollar; and Ecuador, with dollarization. In each case, overvaluation of the currency damaged external competitiveness, reducing the rates of output growth. Eventually, speculation forced depreciation.

More importantly, Chávez generated great expectations about using oil revenues to pay for social programs. His government did indeed implement a massive program of social spending, including an expansion of health assistance and distribution of foodstuffs; social spending as a share of total government spending did go up. Deficits soared, but less as a result of the increase of government spending than as the consequence of lower non-oil revenues due to recession. The social conflicts associated with the political resistance against Chávez exacerbated the fall in non-oil government revenues and forced the government to increase the amount of debt finance. Public debt has soared; interest payments on outstanding debt corresponded to around 40% of total spending [in 2004].

Like Argentina and Brazil, Venezuela has kept substantial primary surpluses—reaching 3% of GDP in 2004—even as its nominal deficits have grown. According to Leonardo Vera, a professor at the Central University of Venezuela, a vicious circle has developed in which reduced revenues lead to more indebtedness, and indebtedness, in turn, leads to higher debt service costs. As this vicious circle turns, wealth is redistributed, but not in the way Chávez hoped—rather, from the poor to the wealthy owners of public bonds.

An Unequal Income Distribution

Across Latin America, governments both center-right and center-left have pursued fiscal policies aimed at containing deficits and trying to reduce the burden of debt. As a result, they have shunned countercyclical spending programs and neglected the effects of fiscal policy on income distribution. The region as a whole obtained a primary surplus of 1% of GDP in 2004, while the nominal deficit was close to 2% of GDP. This means that Latin America, a region of highly unequal income distribution, transferred on average 3% of GDP to the owners of government bonds last year.

With Latin American governments maintaining primary surpluses even in times of crisis and channeling a sizable share of spending into interest payments—in other words, redistributing it to the wealthy—it is not surprising that unemployment remains high across the region. The average rate of unemployment in 2003, according to ECLAC, was above 10%, with Argentina (15%) and Venezuela (18%) heading the charts. As high as these official measures of unemployment are, they underestimate the problems of underemployment and low-productivity jobs typical in the region. These numbers are particularly problematic because leveling the income distribution and reducing unemployment are essential to addressing the region's high poverty rate. Poverty fell in 2004, but not enough to make up for the increase between 2001 and 2003; around 43% of Latin Americans still live below the poverty line. And nothing in the macroeconomic policies of the new left governments suggests that their outcomes are likely to diverge from those in the rest of the region in the coming years.

> "Several countries in Latin America have been laying institutional pillars, and casting monetary and fiscal anchors, without the confines of any ... strict ideology."

Pragmatism, Not Populist Ideology, Drives Latin American Economic Growth

Javier Santiso

In the following viewpoint, Javier Santiso argues that Latin America's economic growth is a pragmatic reaction to social conditions, not populist political ideology. Latin American populist leaders, he asserts, are pursing economic policies that transcend traditional leftist ideological principles. Chile's socialist leader, for example, has privatized pension funds, a policy that is not traditionally socialist. Another example, according to Santiso, is the fiscal conservatism of Brazil's left-leaning president, who has nonetheless kept his promise to support social programs. Santiso is the author of Latin America's Political Economy of the Possible: Beyond Good Revolutionaries and Free-Marketeers *and*

Javier Santiso, "Latin America's New Pragmatism: Unprecedented Stability and Growth Have Taken Hold in Some Major Latin American Countries. The Reasons Are More Original Than They May Seem," *OECD Observer*, May 2006. Copyright © 2006 OECD Publications and Information Centre. Reproduced by permission.

the Director of the Organisation for Economic Co-operation and Development (OECD) Development Centre.

As you read, consider the following questions:

1. In Santiso's opinion, what has enhanced the appeal of anti-globalization policies in Latin America?
2. According to the author, when did Mexico's pragmatic approach to its economy begin?
3. Which Latin American nations does the author think are up to the challenge of steering clear of the rocky shores of their populist sirens?

Latin America is back in the spotlight this year [2006]. The political climate is warming up once again, with major elections taking place in several countries. Economic prospects remain bright, as low interest rates and high prices of raw material exports bolster Asian-style growth rates, while China in particular sucks in huge quantities of soya, iron, copper, oil and gas. The emerging markets are awash in liquidity, with high yields attracting investors. Latin America has recorded three successive years of growth, its first such run in half a century and one that looks set to continue in 2006.

What Lies Beneath

But underneath this impressive performance lies a rather turbulent social and political picture. Global markets may have spurred the growth, but a cocktail of persistent poverty and social discontent have enhanced the popular appeal of anti-globalisation policies. Presidents have been driven out of office in Argentina, Bolivia, Ecuador and Peru, replaced by populist icons such as Bolivia's Evo Morales, an indigenous Indian, leftist and critic of the US.

Latin Americans—and the markets—are divided about this sea of changes. Some see instability and worse poverty ahead. Others see hope and a better, more independent, future. But putting these events into perspective, what really stands out are not so much the popular protests as the profound—and less noisy—domestic transformations that have been taking place in some of the countries of the region over several decades. Indeed, for the last quarter century several countries in Latin America have been laying institutional pillars, and casting monetary and fiscal anchors, without the confines of any predetermined path or strict ideology. Chile is one of those countries, Brazil and Mexico also.

A Bias for Hope

Take Chile first of all. Long held up as a pioneer of economic transformation, Chile again broke new ground in March 2006 when Michelle Bachelet became the first woman president in South America. Yet far from being a radical swing, this significant event reflected Chile's ongoing pragmatism as the socialist leader has promised continuity. In other words, rather than lapsing into *fracasomanía* (failure syndrome) as countries in the region have done in the past, it portrays a widespread optimism, what Albert Hirschman would call a "bias for hope".

Consider for instance the privatisation of pension funds, which in regulatory terms was a jewel of top quality institutional craftsmanship. Launched in the early 1980s, the pension funds produced high yields during the first half of the 1990s, and tried to accommodate the country's low savings rates of barely 20% of GDP [gross domestic product]. Reforms also addressed the informal job markets in a bid to cast the pensions net as widely as possible. The result is that over half of Chile's workers now have coverage, far more than in many other Latin American countries. Moreover, assets are estimated at 71% of GDP ($75 billion in 2005) with strong annual growth.

After the return to democracy in 1989, there might have been a temptation to create yet another model in a euphoric break with the previous military regime. Not a bit of it. Chilean democrats stepped up existing reforms, combining monetary and fiscal orthodoxy with social measures and a drive for balanced growth. In short, the reform is symbolic of the new shift towards pragmatic and gradual transformation after years of dizzying ideologies.

True, the pension system may not be perfect—coverage is still far from universal, and more has to be done to encourage savings and raise normal state pensions, which currently stand at about $130 per month. But the process has allowed healthy long-term capital markets to develop and to reduce Chile's dependence on external financing. The country's pension reforms have even been emulated by several Latin American countries, with varying degrees of success. Little wonder the regulatory body, the Superintendencia, has earned respect as one of the country's most credible and technically accomplished institutions.

The Signs of Pragmatism

There has been pragmatism on the external front too; while Chile opened up its markets and signed free trade agreements with countries all around the world, including Japan, Korea and, lately, China, it nonetheless retained some capital controls (albeit "suspending" them in 1998).

Also, despite widespread privatisation, the country's main company has remained a public one; indeed, Codelco, the copper giant, is a true world leader, providing 30% of the world copper production and 20% of Chilean total exports. This makes it the largest single asset in the country, providing 15% of the national budget and accounting for nearly 5% of GDP.

Mexico's pragmatism kicked in a little later, with the signing of a free trade agreement with the United States and Canada in 1994. Sure enough, the country had already joined the GATT [General Agreement on Tariffs and Trade] and in the same year became the first Latin American member of the

OECD [Organization for Economic Co-operation and Development]. But the North American Free Trade Agreement [NAFTA] marked the first time in history that an emerging economy from the "south" had joined a free trade area with industrialised countries from the "north". It proved to be a test for Mexico, as witness the currency crisis shortly after NAFTA's launch, followed by tough restructuring programmes.

However, the economy came through in the end. In the same way as Spain with the European Union a decade or so earlier, the process was to allow the economy to benefit from a credible anchor on the external side. By 2000, the country had undergone a smooth change of government, for once without sparking a financial crisis—this newly found political normality represented another breakthrough.

Stabilizing Institutions

Mexico can now count on a range of institutional stabilisers, with economic pragmatism becoming the alpha and omega of government policy. While the central bank accumulated more than $70 billon in reserves, Mexico's by now freely floating peso steadied and its inflation rate eased. In fact, by 2005 it reached as low as 3.3%, down from 5.2% a year earlier, its lowest rate in nearly four decades. Public finances are now broadly balanced and Mexico is the only major Latin American country, apart from Chile, to benefit from an investment-grade sovereign credit rating. No one would dream of putting such hard-won stability at risk now, not even Andrés López Obrador, the former mayor of Mexico City and left-wing candidate in the 2006 presidential race, whose recent "market-friendly" regional tour included a stop-off in Wall Street.

The fact that the governor of the politically independent central bank will remain in office until 2009 will help reassure the markets, as will the presence of the Federal Electoral Institute (IFE), another innovation to assure the independent supervision of democratic elections. Future governments will

Working Together to Promote Just Economic Policies

While the populism vs. pragmatism thesis has falsely portrayed an internally divided left, Latin America's progressive leaders have never been closer. Lula, Kirchner and Bachelet have all, on several occasions, defended Chávez against U.S. criticism. . . .

Assessing the Latin left on the basis of its actual policies reveals an entirely different picture than the one painted by mainstream U.S. media outlets. U.S. policy makers should refrain from buying into such alarmist and paranoid rhetoric and judging the Latin left on ideological grounds alone. Latin America's shift to the left is a symptom of the tremendous unpopularity and failure of U.S. policies in the region. . . .

Unjust social and economic policies can only be perpetuated through violence and repression. Today, the people of Latin America are once again standing up against injustice and U.S. hegemony.

Juan Antonio Montecino,
"Cleaving a False Divide in Latin America,"
Foreign Policy in Focus,
September 28, 2006. www.fpif.org.

have the tough job of tackling such challenges as widespread poverty and furthering the structural changes needed to help Mexico close the gap with its OECD partners. But on the whole, the economic and institutional scene is set for the winner of the 2006 elections to uphold pragmatic reforms and so help Mexico step up its remarkable transformation of the last decade.

The Brazilian Story

The Brazilian story is different. In fact, after much promise and several false starts, the financial markets became nervous in 2002 with [Luiz Inácio] Lula's rise to power, but were in the end pleasantly surprised by the left-wing president's attachment to the monetary and fiscal orthodoxy of the previous administrations. In 2004, Lula managed to bring the country's economic growth rate to around 5%. At the same time, as for Chile and Mexico, he looked to trade to anchor the transformation process. Even though the exchange rate appreciated by almost 15% in 2005, the trade surplus reached a record $45 billion, as total exports broke the $100 billion barrier for the second year running.

The momentum for change has been powerful and several important fiscal, pension and banking reforms have withstood the test of parliament. Lula's social programmes and investment in infrastructure, though much criticised, have not damaged the new found fiscal and monetary orthodoxy. Moreover, Lula has attempted to stick to promises of more just, efficient and equitable growth.

He has raised the minimum wage and tried to boost social programmes in education and health. His fight against hunger may also be working, with a reduction of poverty recorded [in 2004 and 2005] by the local-based research institution, Getulio Vargas Foundation. Whether Lula is to be re-elected again in 2006 is an open question, but pragmatism seems to be so well anchored now that whoever wins . . . will probably not change course. [Lula was reelected in October 2006.]

Rather than engaging in impossible strategies, the trio of Chile, Mexico and Brazil have used the art of the possible to deliver change. Will these experiences inspire the rest of Latin America to set their compasses and sail clear of the rocky shores and their populist sirens? Some are up to the challenge, Uruguay for instance, where a left-wing government claiming this new pragmatism has also come to power. But in Bolivia,

Ecuador and Venezuela, clearly the signals point in the opposite direction. Nevertheless, . . . while it remains to be seen which trend gains the upper hand, the chances are that Latin America's new wave of pragmatism will not fade just yet.

> *"Privatization has meant higher rates, lower quality, less access, and less sovereign control over public services."*

Privatization Increases Economic Inequality in Latin America

Jason Wallach

In the following viewpoint, Jason Wallach maintains that several Latin American leaders have turned once public businesses over to the private sector because some economists believe that privatization makes businesses more efficient and promotes economic growth. Unfortunately, Wallach argues, many privatized Latin American businesses, including public utilities, are not running more efficiently or improving the economy. In fact, he states, privatization has led to the loss of many jobs. While public businesses still face problems, Wallach asserts, they are at least accountable to the people. Wallach writes for the NACLA News, *a publication of the North American Congress on Latin America.*

As you read, consider the following questions:

1. What example does Wallach provide of a private utility gone wrong?

Jason Wallach, "El Salvador: Water Inc. and the Criminalization of Protest," *NACLA News*, July 24, 2007. Copyright © 2007 NACLA. Reproduced by permission.

2. In what other industries in El Salvador has privatization failed, according to El Salvadoran water union (SETA) members cited by Wallach?

3. What political message is the government sending by jailing those who protest privatization, according to Julio César Portillo, husband of a jailed protestor, as quoted by Wallach?

When residents in Santa Eduviges [El Salvador] entered their second month without running water [in 2006], everyone knew something had to be done. A town assembly was called. Community members expressed outrage that the water company's $7 per month bill always arrived on time, but taps barely flowed. When they did, the liquid that came out was an ugly brown.

In the assembly, anger quickly turned toward system operator Roberto Saprissa. He received the money, but was doing nothing to fix the system's problems. They complained that service under Saprissa was deficient and polluted. Despite a number of meetings with government officials, the company simply did not respond.

Protesting Privatization

The community discussed the issue and came to a decision. They demanded the de-privatization of the town water system and its management to be put under the control of the national water agency, ANDA (Administración Nacional de Acueductos y Alcantarillados).

Days later, residents of this small community near the San Salvador suburb of Soyapango, overtook the Gold Highway that leads into the capital. Young and old occupied the busy thoroughfare from the morning rush until 6 p.m. The community made their demand clear: "Give us clean water and put our system under government control." That evening, police fired tear gas to dislodge the crowd and arrested five people.

The Backlash Against Privatization

Across Latin America, a growing number of people say the privatization of public services, a movement that swept the region in the 1980s and 1990s, has failed. Protests have erupted over the issue in several countries, and some governments are beginning to reverse these policies. . . .

The backlash against the private sector has been building for several years in many pockets of the region. In some cases, such as Bolivia and Mexico, it has been actively promoted by grassroots leaders in tandem with their demands for limiting the influence of foreign interests.

Monte Reel, "Turning the Taps Back to the States:
Privatization of Utilities Falls Out of Favor in Latin America,"
Washington Post Foreign Service, *March 27, 2006.*

Eventually the government dropped the charges and released the five residents arrested during the protests. The community won a rare victory: the water system was put firmly under government control. But all that may soon change.

While dozens of communities in El Salvador have occupied roads demanding water service, the particular conflict that confronted this village of 300 people—and their unusual demand—stands to be repeated now that right-wing deputies in El Salvador's Legislative Assembly are threatening to pass a controversial General Water Law. The legislation calls for water administration to shift from the national to the municipal level and requires local governments to sign over water management through "concessions"—or contracts with private firms—for up to 50 years. The proposed law has become a lightning rod for opposition from community groups and social organizations who say it amounts to a privatization of the country's water system.

Private vs. Public Water Management

Critics of privatization argue that keeping the water under state-management through the ANDA is the lesser among various evils. The national entity is mired in corruption and bribery scandals and has been the target of extreme budget cuts by Salvadoran President Antonio Saca. Its budget was slashed 15% in 2005, falling to its lowest level this decade—a perplexing reduction in a country where 40% of rural Salvadorans have no access to potable water.

While it is clear that the state-run ANDA isn't the smoothest-sailing ship in the sea, many believe it remains the most accessible and accountable entity for communities with an urgent need for water. ANDA workers responsible for repairing water systems agree. They say they want to work, but accuse the government of engaging a plan to discredit the agency and thus, justify the privatization as a solution to poor service.

"People complain about ANDA's slow response time," says Wilfredo Romero, General Secretary at SETA, the union of ANDA workers. "But delays don't happen because workers don't want to work; we do. But to make repairs, we need an assignment order from management."

Those orders, charges SETA's International Relations Secretary Jorge René Cordoba, "are prioritized for systems that are planned to be concessioned off. The rest have to wait their turn." SETA members explain that municipalities who reject water concessions are put at the end of the line. As a result, service has slowed to a crawl in San Salvador, where Mayor Violeta Menjívar from the FMLN political party opposes concessioning the city's water services.

SETA took out half-page ads in the nation's two biggest daily newspapers opposing the General Water Law, which according to the ad, "would privatize water and condemn thousands of our compatriots to suffer thirst for the inability to pay."

Privatization Failures

SETA members point to the devastating results of the recent privatizations of the country's telecommunications and electricity sectors, which led to the firing of thousands of workers. Many of these workers were forced to re-apply for the same jobs at half the pay with none of the state-provided benefits. The average ANDA worker currently makes about $300 [per] month.

"If we take the electricity sector and telecommunications as guides, privatization has meant higher rates, lower quality, less access, and less sovereign control over public services," says Krista Hanson of the Committee in Solidarity with the People of El Salvador (CISPES).

Privately run water concessions in Latin America have a terrible track record. The most notorious example occurred with a project imposed by the World Bank in Cochabamba, Bolivia. The Bank made delivery of a loan conditional on the privatization of the country's largest water systems. When the Cochabamba water services concession ran by the U.S.-based Bechtel Corporation raised household water bills by 200%, it sparked a civil uprising that forced the company to leave the country and the water system was put under public control. After Cochabamba, the World Bank retired the word "privatization" and replaced it with terms like "concessions" and "decentralization," or "private sector participation." But critics say whatever the euphemism, the end result is the same: higher rates, lower quality, and less access.

New Words, Same Problems

In El Salvador the Inter-American Development Bank (IDB), a division of the World Bank, approved loan 0068-ES, "Reform Program For the Water Sector and the Potable Water and Sanitation Sub-sector" in 1998. The main function of the loan was to transfer state-run water companies "under a decentralization of services with private sector participation." The IDB directed $36 million of the loan for the "promotion of such private sector participation (PSP) using specialized consultants to give support and financial advice to the government towards the effective organization of PSP schemes."

It was one of these new "schemes" President Saca planned to announce on July 2 [2007] in Suchitoto 28 miles northeast of San Salvador. The speech was meant to inaugurate a "national decentralization policy," including water administration. Saca arrived by helicopter and was quickly shuffled off in a limo to an elite resort area on Lake Suchitoto to make his announcement, but hundreds of invited dignitaries, including the Japanese Ambassador never got there. Road blockades guarded by unionists, grassroots organizations and community residents against the plan prevented their arrival.

Militarized police swat teams attacked the peaceful protestors with tear gas and rubber bullets. Among the 14 people arrested, were Marta Lorena Araujo and Rosa Maria Centeno the president and vice-president, respectively, of the Association for the Development of El Salvador (CRIPDES), a widely respected grassroots organization.

Araujo, Centeno and two other CRIPDES representatives rode in a red pick-up truck toward the protest in Suchitoto when police pulled them over and arrested them near the community of Milingo.

The driver was accused with assaulting a police officer, though footage of his arrest proves he put up no resistance to the needlessly aggressive officers. "More than anything, this was a kidnapping," charged Julio César Portillo, husband of the jailed Araujo. "With it, the government is sending a political message: 'Don't protest.'"

The Perils of Protest

Charges of "Acts of Terrorism" will stand against thirteen of the fourteen defendants. Judge Ana Lucila Fuentes de Paz of the Special Tribunal of San Salvador also denied bail for the jailed activists, who will have to wait up to 90 days in El Salvador's notoriously harsh and crowded jails while prosecutors gather evidence for trial.

Fuentes de Paz threw out "Public Disorder" and "Illicit Association" charges against all the defendants, because prosecutors failed to provide evidence. A fourteenth defendant, Facundo García, had all charges dropped. Fuentes said García had only sought to aid those being arrested, which did not constitute a crime. After more than two weeks in jail, a review panel of judges allowed the conditional release of four more defendants on July 20 [2007], but the charges against them still stand.

The "Suchitoto 13" are being charged with "terrorism" through the draconian "Special Law Against Acts of Terrorism" (SLAAT) passed after a sniper killed two police officers during a protest in July [2006]. Activists say the application of the SLAAT confirms their warnings that the law would be used to criminalize protest and silence dissent. Amnesty International decisively condemned the detentions: "[Amnesty] fears the detentions were carried out to punish people for participating in the legitimate protests and to inhibit similar acts in the future."

Demonstrations erupted against the detentions with protesters calling the 13 detainees El Salvador's first political prisoners since Peace Accords were signed in 1992. A July 4 [2007] statement signed by more than 60 Salvadoran social organizations demanded an immediate release of all detainees. Barring that, they exhorted respect for the physical integrity of the accused by state authorities. The demands were made in the wake of reports police had threatened to throw some detainees out of a transport helicopter as it hung over Lake Suchitoto the day of the arrests. Such threats resonate deeply here, with state-sponsored human rights atrocities of the civil war still fresh in people's minds.

| "The increased nationalism is sad in light of the fact that state has never been a good driver of growth and development in Latin America."

State Control of Industry Restricts Economic Growth in Latin America

Latin Business Chronicle

In the following viewpoint, the editors of Latin Business Chronicle *maintain that efforts by some Latin American leaders to nationalize industry threaten economic growth in the region. Nationalization, they argue, will discourage foreign investors. Not only does foreign investment lead to more jobs, according to the authors, it also increases access to technology and expertise, all of which are sacrificed when an industry is nationalized. Latin American governments have never been good at driving economic growth or managing national companies, the editors conclude.* Latin Business Chronicle *is an online source for Latin American business news.*

Latin Business Chronicle, "Latin America's Nationalist Mistakes," January 8, 2007. Reproduced by permission.

As you read, consider the following questions:

1. What did Bolivian President Evo Morales say to justify the nationalization of the energy sector in his country?

2. According to *Latin Business Chronicle*, why has CANTV become an efficient and successful communications operator?

3. In the authors' view, what will ensure sustained growth, lasting jobs, and declines in poverty in Latin America?

In Venezuela, President Hugo Chavez . . . declared that he plans to nationalize the country's telecommunications and electricity sectors, a measure that will affect private companies like CANTV [a Venezuelan telecommunications company].

"All those sectors that are so strategic, such as electric power, everything that was privatized will be nationalized," Chavez said today in a televised speech in Caracas. "We will recover the strategic means of production. CANTV, let's nationalize it," he said, according to a transcript by Bloomberg.

A Pattern of Nationalization

The decision to nationalize CANTV comes after Chavez bullied the private company into retroactively raising the pensions of former workers. It also follows earlier decisions to raise royalties on foreign oil companies and restrict new mining activity to the Venezuelan state.

In Bolivia, the country's energy minister says he wants to raise taxes sixfold on mining, a measure that would hurt Canadian mining companies like Eaglecrest Explorations and Orvana Minerals Corp. That follows the May 2006 nationalization of the energy sector. "The neo-liberal governments gave away hills, rivers and mining concessions. We have to start recovering those concessions," Bolivian President Evo Morales said in a speech today, according to Reuters.

In Ecuador, the outgoing government expropriated the operations of U.S. oil giant Occidental and increased govern-

A Self-Defeating Strategy

Jeff Rosensweig, a professor of finance at Emory University's Goizueta Business School, agrees [that government-run industry is inefficient and will lead to more poverty]. "Throughout the world, the weight of the evidence has shown that nationalization of industries leads to inefficiency," he says. "First, nationalization causes a drain of foreign investment that could bring in new technology, management techniques, and capital needed to modernize the industry. Second, nationalization often displaces talented executives who are experienced with political cronies appointed to replace them."

In Venezuela, for instance, he says, many talented professionals have been pushed out, and have left for Miami, Florida. "Therefore, although the idea of nationalizing a private industry is seductive, it ultimately is self-defeating as it proves costly to a nation that thinks it will be a strategy for economic development," he contends.

Knowledge@Emory,
"Is Nationalization a Good Strategy for Latin America?" 2007.

ment royalties on oil production from 20 to 50 percent. Even in Peru, where a "pragmatic" Alan Garcia won the elections last year, authorities have imposed new taxes and fees on the mining sector.

And in Argentina, President Nestor Kirchner practically expelled French utility giant Suez so the water sector could be run by an inefficient state company.

The government policies come on top of growing protests against foreign investors, especially in the mining sector, where critics are demanding a share of the profits from the recent commodity boom.

A Counter-Productive Strategy

All this nationalism is counter-productive. Yes, the profits of oil and mining companies have grown as the international prices of those products has increased. But that's the cycle of the markets. The two sectors also see periods of price reductions and losses.

Punishing the foreign investors in mining and oil in the good times will only lead them to reduce their investments in Latin America, a region that desperately needs more—not less—foreign and private investments.

Just as important as investments that expand facilities and operations, creating direct and indirect jobs, is the transfer of technology and know-how. Latin America lags significantly behind Asia in this area and thus benefits greatly when foreign multinationals share their expertise and even create local research and development centers.

Foreign investors also have been able to train a new breed of Latin American executives, that go on to work for the company outside of Latin America or even start their own companies locally. They have gained from a keen understanding of global competition, much more than they would if they worked for a politicized and mediocre state company.

The CANTV Example

Then there's the case of CANTV, the inefficient Venezuelan state telecom that was privatized in 1991. Thanks to private management, the company (Venezuela's largest private company) has become a highly efficient and successful operator. It is operated and partly owned by US-based telecom giant Verizon, but was scheduled to be sold to a joint venture of

Mexico-based America Movil and Telmex (which have the same owner). The Mexicans were going to buy Verizon's 28.5 percent stake for $676.6 million to begin with, then eventually buy up shares. The public and institutional investors own 58.2 percent of the remaining shares, while the government of Venezuela owns 6.6 percent and CANTV employees and retirees own 6.7 percent, according to the Yankee Group.

The deal was originally expected [in 2006], but repeatedly delayed due to the Venezuelan government postponing their final approval. Now we know why. CANTV was never going to be sold to Telmex or any one else, but form part of the new superstate in Venezuela (which also runs airlines and produces PCs and tractors in addition to the increasingly inefficient state oil company PDVSA). Coupled with Chavez' plans to create one big political party, close opposition media and be able to govern indefinitely and Venezuela is looking eerily like Cuba in the 1960s.

The increased nationalism is sad in light of the fact that state has never been a good driver of growth and development in Latin America nor a good administrator of companies, which instead typically are overbloated, inefficient and moneylosing operations.

Just as statist, populist policies failed in Latin America when they were tried in the 1970s, they will fail again today. Instead of restricting foreign investment, Latin American governments need to welcome them with open arms. Only pro-investment policies will ensure sustained growth, lasting jobs and real poverty declines.

| "Corruption reduces investment incentives, increases transaction costs, and results in reduced economic growth."

Internal Corruption Weakens Latin American Economies

Edward L. Cleary

In the following viewpoint, Edward L. Cleary argues that corruption reduces economic growth in Latin America, often at the expense of the most vulnerable populations. Favors given to Latin American elites in return for foreign development projects benefit the rich, not the economy, he maintains. Bribes taken by police and bureaucrats not only lead to unequal treatment and coercion, but they also reduce the supply of resources, Cleary asserts. Fighting corruption in Latin America will therefore improve the region's economic prospects, he reasons. Cleary is director of Latin American Studies at Providence College and has served as a missionary in Bolivia and Peru.

As you read, consider the following questions:

1. According to Cleary, why has corruption only recently become a priority for those who monitor human rights violations in Latin America?

Edward L. Cleary, "New Priority for Churches and Missions: Combating Corruption," *International Bulletin of Missionary Research*, vol. 31, October 2007, pp. 182–185. Copyright © 2006 Overseas Ministries Study Center. Reproduced by permission.

2. Why has Latin America become a movement society, in the author's opinion?

3. In the author's view, what do some students and readers learn about Latin America that often comes as a surprise?

The International Conference on Combating Corruption, sponsored by the Pontifical Council for Justice and Peace, was held at Rome in June 2006. Eighty experts from around the world attended, as did seventeen ambassadors of various countries accredited to the Holy See. It was the first such conference, but it was not the opening bell in a new fight. Rather, it was recognition of what has been going on for the last few years at the grassroots and national levels.

I attended this conference, which gave me an opportunity to compare efforts at combating corruption taking place in other regions with those in Latin America. I came away believing that Latin America has made good progress in this effort. Furthermore, corruption clearly is an issue at the top of the agenda for groups and churches devoted to concern for the poor.

A Priority Shift

Corruption has become a priority for monitors of human rights violations in Latin America. This evil would not have been listed twenty years ago, when death and disappearance were the focus of human rights groups. This is not an isolated fight issuing only from the grassroots; Latin American governments acknowledge corruption as a key issue. Furthermore, the United Nations, the Organization of American States, the World Bank, and the Latin American Catholic Church have thrown their weight behind the struggle. In this [viewpoint] I address why this shift occurred and how the issue pertains to human rights.

Corruption has affected Latin America for centuries. But now, along with some other regions of the world, Latin American human rights groups have made corruption a special target. In a word, corruption has increased in scale because of new opportunities, but so too have efforts to combat it. Since the mid-1990s the Catholic Church—especially in the person of one of its main leaders, Cardinal Oscar Rodriguez, archbishop of Tegucigalpa, Honduras—has thrown its weight behind this struggle.

The New Intolerance for Corruption

During the 1980s and 1990s many Latin American countries were turning to democracy after military or other forms of authoritarian rule. It then became clear that it would not be corruption as usual. In the largest country, Brazil, President Fernando Collor de Mello was impeached in 1992 on corruption charges, which led to his resignation. As far as one could recall, this was the first president in the history of Latin America to be removed through the impeachment process. Public opinion and human rights groups are credited with forcing a timid Congress to vote through the impeachment.

This act would have gone as a curiosity in history if similar proceedings had not taken place in 1993 against Jorge Serrano Elias in Guatemala and Carlos Andres Perez in Venezuela. Over the next dozen years Peru, Ecuador, and Bolivia forced presidents to resign because of abuse of power. In the mid-1990s Mexico saw its once-strong president Carlos Salinas de Gotari go off into exile after it became clear that he and his family had enriched themselves through corruption. In Nicaragua, former president Arnoldo Aleman probably wished he had gone into exile in 2002 instead of fighting proceedings that in times past he would have won but in the new era brought him a twenty-year prison sentence for fraud and embezzlement. In Argentina, speculators say Carlos Menem guessed right by dropping out of the presidential race in 2003 after winning the first round, since there was evidence of wrongdoing in secret arms deals with Ecuador. The list of the disgraced presidents may grow, now that even Costa Rica's typically clean presidents may turn out to be tainted.

The Impact of Globalization

How could even Costa Rica, which ranks so well on Transparency International's ranking of corruption practices, have three former presidents be accused of corruption? Or how could Salinas and family in Mexico be thought to have gone off with something like US$120 million?

At the Rome conference, all agreed on the major point that the globalization of national economies in the form it had taken in the previous fifteen years had offered new opportunities for enrichment. Not only did a globalized economy in general bring large opportunities for illicit enrichment, but national institutional sources of corruption increased in post-authoritarian situations. Transnational sources of investment money and "favors" added new and often secret sources of enrichment. The size of development projects meant that billions of dollars were available.

Privatization was an especially vexing opportunity for enrichment. Latin American economies, for the most part, were statist. The state sold off public enterprises, such as television networks, phone companies, and public utilities, through a corruptible process of privatization. It was not always clear at what price and to whom they were sold. When governments divested themselves of telephone companies, airlines, television stations, and other enterprises, it was likened in Mexico to la pinata, a birthday party game with a papier-mache figure. The figure, whose belly is filled with candy, is broken by a blow of a stick, and the goodies fall at the feet of the invited few, who scoop up the favors. So too were Mexican fortunes made by the favored in-crowd. Sometimes foreigners were the favored beneficiaries, as when Venezuela cut loose CANTV [a telecommunications company], Viasa airline, and several large hotels at undervalued prices in the 1980s.

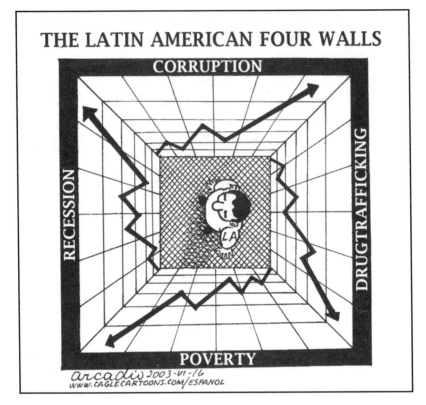

"The Latin American Four Walls," cartoon by Arcadio Esquivel. Copyright © 2003 by Arcadio Esquivel and CagleCartoons.com. All rights reserved.

The Process of Democratization

Latin American reactions in facing up to corruption, however, are also new. Most of the countries are recent democracies, forged out of reaction to military or authoritarian dictatorship. Latin America was part of what in political science has been called the third wave of democratization. Churches, Catholic and Protestant, were in the forefront of this effort to turn societies into democracies. So too were churches major advocates for human rights both during and after military dictatorships. Besides the involvement of some of the great figures of twentieth-century Christianity—persons such as Oscar Romero and Medardo Gomez, Catholic and Lutheran bishops of El Salvador—very large numbers of Christians filled the ranks of human rights groups formerly against military abuses and now against corruption.

In the process of democratization, major debates on the shape of future governance took place. Perhaps for the first time, many persons began to believe that a way forward with lessened corruption was possible. In part this belief was based on seeing what their own actions could accomplish. In the 1980s and 1990s they created better neighborhoods, forced the government to be more responsive to their needs, and advocated and advanced basic human rights. In a word, Latin America had become in many places a movement society or at least had the makings of a civil society it did not possess, say, in 1970. Evidence shows that there are some one million civil society organizations in Latin America. Many of them are devoted to improving good governance and thereby the lives of ordinary people at the grass roots. Many participants in these groups are or have been members of small Christian communities. One could find here parallels with the anticorruption movement in the Philippines that seems to be intimately tied to Christian Base Communities. In Latin America, however, the membership of groups working against corruption is highly diverse.

People at the grass roots now have a twenty- to thirty-year history of activism that includes some impressive accomplishments. A longtime observer of Brazil found a sense of achievement in activists who had seen their work consistently advance despite harsh repression and setbacks. In Chile, Argentina, Bolivia, and Peru I observed similar vital debates and was struck by the number of late-teens and twenty-year-olds assuming full membership in the social activist groups. The age-replacement factor for leadership is also positive in Brazil's largest sociopolitical movement, the Movement of the Landless Rural Workers (MST). . . .

Viewing Corruption

Corruption is not a formless evil on the science-fiction channel. At the level of the ordinary citizen, corruption takes shape as the request, often implicit but well understood, for payment of a fee to officials for services rendered or penalties avoided. Police, school staff, and government bureaucrats receiving poverty-level wages hoped to be aided toward a more reasonable level of income by receiving mordida (the bite) or muneca (money placed under the wristwatch or bracelet), to mention but two of many colorful names for this practice.

It often comes as a surprise to students and to readers to learn that some academics find that corruption can serve good purposes. None did at the Rome conference, but several serious scholars, including Harvard's Samuel Huntington, have defended the idea that there are positive aspects of bribes and other kinds of corruption. They have affirmed that bribes are like stimulants, making sluggish bureaucracies act when they otherwise would not have acted, even in a good cause.

The Economic Impact of Corruption

None of the Rome participants were in a mood for such speculation. Since half of the participants were laypersons working in transnational organizations, governmental agencies, or NGOs [nongovernmental organizations], they, along with their clerical colleagues, were in agreement about the starting point of the conference: corruption steals from the poor. Estimates of the scope of this theft reach into the trillions of dollars.

Furthermore, economists point out that corruption reduces investment incentives, increases transaction costs, and results in reduced economic growth. In one of the most extensive efforts to estimate bribery costs for one aspect of corruption—government services—grassroots pollsters interviewed heads of households. The investigators estimated that corruption in the use of public services cost Bolivians, most of them very poor, the equivalent of US$115 million a year. The survey included a full range of forty-two public services. Each household was estimated as having paid $50 a year in bribes, a sum equal to 90 percent of a monthly salary. No wonder, then, that economists at the World Bank have identified corruption as the single greatest obstacle to economic and social development.

Political scientists more recently have argued that corruption erodes the legitimacy of governments, the major pillar of democracy. Through extensive research in nine countries, [Vanderbilt University's] Mitchell Seligson showed that corruption does erode the legitimacy of governance, a precious commodity in the new democracies of Latin America. Legitimacy is needed for the stability of governmental systems. Human rights activists have argued that corruption in government basically steals from the poor the resources that should be going into provision for their healthcare, education, and other services. . . .

For the most part, the perspective of economists and older political scientists tends to focus on the institutional level, as budget accountability. In contrast, human rights activists, the church, and, more recently, younger political scientists have emphasized the individual and the resources that institutions are supposed to dispense to persons without coercion.

The Victims of Corruption

Mitchell Seligson has explored one aspect of the personal perspective: the individual as victim of corruption. A political scientist working originally at the University of Pittsburgh and now at Vanderbilt University, Seligson created the Latin American Public Opinion Project (LAPOP) to report on opinion polls he conducted. This research brought an empirical perspective that went beyond the endless essays about Latin American corruption.

Through tireless public opinion polling especially in Mexico, Colombia, and seven other countries of Latin America, Seligson and his collaborators conducted research into those who have been directly affected by corrupt transactions. In 2004 they focused on corruption-victimization in the workplace and in four government services: health, courts, schools, and local government. This valuable research yielded information about the frequency with which bribes occurred and about the venues in which they occurred.

In some ways the results they provide are both better and worse than one might have expected. Some countries, such as war-torn Colombia, have a good deal fewer victims of corruption than other countries, and the overall averages for the nine countries are probably a good deal better than for many developing countries. However, to find that the school system is the venue for the most bribery was shocking to Seligson, as it would probably be to most observers. One hates to dwell on the implications of children being socialized in systems where corruption is endemic. (In the worst case, Ecuador, almost one in four parents reported paying school bribes.) Municipal bribery was almost as high as school bribery and court bribery, followed by lower rates of bribery in the workplace and in health services. The percentages ranged from 10.6 percent of Latin Americans who were victims of school bribery to 7.5 percent who reported being asked for health-service bribes.

Variations Among Nations

The differences among countries were significant. Among the nine countries studied, Mexicans and Ecuadorans were subjected to more corruption than citizens of the other seven. Regarding all kinds of bribes, one-fifth of the Mexican population experienced some form of bribery; Ecuadorans experienced almost the same level. In other countries, only from 3 to 10 percent said they were similarly approached.

Seligson's results make clear the effect of corruption. In contrast to receiving fair and equal distribution of goods from the state and free and uncoerced delivery of service from public servants, citizens receive unjust treatment and coercion. Corruption thus strikes at the heart of the rule of law and due process, which are the foundations of democracy. Furthermore, corruption induces a fear that is a kind of low-level terrorism or at least a coercion that reduces the kind of trust needed to oil the workings of good governance. A case could be made that police and bureaucrats are also victims in the sense that they do not receive income from wages sufficient to support themselves and their families. Bribes, slightly similar to tips to waiters, are seen as part of their wages, perhaps rewarding the zealous officers more than the lazy ones. Beyond the interpersonal aspects, governmental corruption also reduces the supply of resources for all and hurts most the weak and vulnerable. The billions of pesos that have been funneled into private hands is indeed grand theft from the people.

Periodical Bibliography

The following articles have been selected to supplement the diverse views presented in this chapter.

Sarah Anderson	"Foreign Investors Gone Wild," *Foreign Policy in Focus*, May 7, 2007.
Economist	"A Coming Test of Virtue; Latin America's Economies," April 12, 2008.
Economist	"Commerce Between Friends and Foes: Latin America and the United States," October 6, 2007.
Joen Kellberg	"Pragmatism vs. Populism in South America," *Commentary & Analysis*, October 11, 2006.
Juan Antonio Montecino	"Cleaving a False Divide in Latin America," *Foreign Policy in Focus*, September 28, 2006.
Nancy Price	"Water Justice and Democracy: From Dream to Reality," *Peace and Freedom*, Fall 2007.
Alejandro Reuss	"Anti-Neoliberal Backlash: Leaving the World Bank and IMF Behind," *NACLA Report on the Americas*, July/August 2007.
Emir Sader	"The Weakest Link? Neoliberalism in Latin America," *New Left Review*, July/August 2008.
Anoop Singh	"Latin America's Resurgence and the Role of the IMF," *Emerging Markets*, April 3, 2006.
Mark Weisbrot	"The IMF's Dwindling Fortunes," *Los Angeles Times*, April 27, 2008.
Wilson Quarterly	"The Lagging Continent," Winter 2007.

CHAPTER 2

What Is the Political Climate in Latin America?

Chapter Preface

Democracy expanded in Latin America during the late 1980s and 1990s. Despite promises of economic prosperity, however, stark income inequality remains. "Indeed," claims journalist Peter Katel in "Change in Latin America" in *CQ Researcher* (July 21, 2006), "70 percent of Latin America's more than 500 million people live on $300 or less per month." Voters across the region have been calling for change. In fact, bitterness over what many Latin Americans believe to be the failure of U.S.-sponsored free-market economic policies in the region have, in the eyes of many, increased the power of populist leaders. One of the most controversial of these leaders, Venezuela's President Hugo Chávez, came to power in 1998. Since that time, his hostile rhetoric toward the George W. Bush administration has led many to question his leadership. Some claim, however, that Chávez is more bark than bite. "Chávez is not going to deny his people $2 million to $4 million a day of additional revenue just to stick it to the U.S.," maintains Fadel Gheit, chief petroleum analyst at Oppenheimer & Co., a U.S. investment firm. Nevertheless, many analysts debate whether Chávez is a prophetic leader or a dangerous demagogue.

To the poor, who prior to his election were receiving little of the wealth from Venezuela's oil, Chávez is a hero. In addition to bringing Cuban doctors to Venezuela's slums and improving access to water, Chávez has committed billions to programs to improve conditions throughout the Latin American region. For example, Chávez has devoted $10 billion to a Latin America-wide anti-poverty program. He is also using his nation's oil revenues to promote Brazilian energy projects and Bolivian social welfare programs. Chávez helped former President Néstor Kirchner of Argentina pay off his debt to the International Monetary Fund (IMF), which eliminated the IMF's influence over Argentina's economy. According to Chávez, his goal is to solve the problem of inequality in Latin America. "Let's change the model; let's leave capitalism behind. . . . [L]et's go forward to a new kind of socialism, a 21st-century socialism; a model for equality and for justice," Chávez has proclaimed.

Some analysts believe, however, that Chávez is more interested in power than social equality. Teodoro Petkoff, his opponent in the August 2006 primary election in Venezuela, asserts that Chávez's administration is "essentially personality-dominated, with strong traits of militarism, messianism and authoritarianism." Chávez has indeed delegated over $3 billion to purchase arms from Russia and Spain. In fact, some commentators fear that Chávez's anti-American sentiments are more than just rhetoric. Jorge G. Castañeda, professor and foreign minister to Mexico's former president Vicente Fox, maintains that Chávez "is attempting, with some success, to split the hemisphere into two camps: one pro-Chávez, one pro-American." Picking public fights with leaders such as Fox and former President George W. Bush, "is about as close to traditional Latin American populism as one can get—and as far from a modern and socially minded left as one can be," Castañeda claims.

Some scholars contend that Chávez's influence is fading while others argue that the region is moving towards increased national economic policies, independent of U.S. influence. The role Chávez plays in Latin America's political climate indeed remains controversial. The authors in the following chapter explore other controversies in answer to the question surrounding the political climate in Latin America.

| "Latin America is basically peaceful,
stable and well-governed."

Democracy Is Growing in Latin America

John Barham

In the following viewpoint, John Barham argues that despite re-ports to the contrary, democracy is growing in Latin America. For example, he asserts, democratic institutions, such as confi-dent legislatures and independent judiciaries, have grown in strength. Moreover, Latin American institutions have begun tackling crime and corruption, Barham notes. Democratically elected governments are focusing on the needs of the people, spending money on reducing poverty and improving health and education, he maintains. A renewed focus on accountability will lead to even greater growth and reduce inequality, according to Barham. Barham is editor-in-chief of LatinFinance, *an online news source that provides financial markets intelligence for Latin America and the Caribbean.*

As you read, consider the following questions:

1. What has been the impact of connectivity in Latin America, according to Barham?

John Barham, "Two Steps Forward," *LatinFinance*, February 2006, pp. 47–48. Copyright © 2006 Euromoney Institutional Investor PLC. Reproduced by permission.

2. How is economic reform transforming the region, in the author's view?

3. In the author's opinion, why are Argentina's Néstor Kirchner and Venezuela's Hugo Chavez so popular?

I started editing [*LatinFinance*] six years ago. The dawn of the new millennium also saw the rise of the Internet, continued consolidation of democracy in Latin America and the triumph of the Washington Consensus. [The Washington Consensus, also known as neoliberalism, requires deregulating markets, liberalizing trade and finance, and privatizing public business.] A new era of peace, progress and stability was upon us.

We know better now. The experts failed to spot one of history's greatest speculative bubbles. We were blindsided by the rise of China and India, and stunned by the depth of Argentina's collapse. And few predicted the resurgence of virulent populism across Latin America. All true, yet *LatinFinance* told a somewhat different story as it recorded in painstaking detail the zigzags of the region's markets and economic fortunes. We reported that on the whole, Latin America made surprising progress.

That will surprise those who think Latin America has achieved nothing since the dawn of the millennium and that it's doomed to remain a backwater of a globalized economy.

A Positive Picture

Latin America has emerged from its long malaise in fair shape. Government finances are robust and macroeconomic rationality prevails, so the next global economic downturn need not necessarily trigger another Latin American financial crisis. Many Latin Americans, sick of inflation, debased currencies and crooked state-controlled economies, support market economics, even if they are—rightly—unhappy with the execution of government policies. Democracy is well entrenched in the region, except for Cuba, Venezuela and to some extent Ecuador and Nicaragua. The region is at peace—except for Colombia, which is more a victim of the world's craving for illegal drugs than its own violent history. The institutional foundations of a modern state—assertive legislatures, independent judiciaries that enforce the rule of law, autonomous central banks—are growing stronger. Nuclear weapons, megalomaniacal dictators, violent separatism and religious conflict are unknown. Unlike other parts of the developing world, Latin America is basically peaceful, stable and well-governed.

This may not describe the Latin America you think you know. It is true that crime, kidnappings, corruption, ignorance, bureaucracy and poverty are widespread. Although there is plenty of corruption and crime everywhere, Latin Americans are starting to tackle these centuries-old problems. What's more, changes around the world are deepening and accelerating new attitudes that will transform societies across the Americas.

Think about the impact of connectivity. Fixed phone lines were a middle-class luxury a decade ago, but 30%–40% of Latin Americans now have cell phones. About 13% of Latin American households have Internet connections, about four times more than in 2000. Broadband connections are also growing. In Brazil, 4%–5% of homes have broadband service, and 13% will be connected by 2008. E-mail, blogging, vlogging, Internet radio, and even cell-phone cameras are all democratizing the media. These are profoundly liberating phenomena because control of information empowers ordinary people.

Improving the Quality of Politics

Sure, democracy works better in some places than others. Chile and Uruguay are the only Latin American countries with the highest rankings for political rights and civil liberties from Freedom House [an international organization promoting democratic values], but most of the main countries have reasonably high scores. For the first time in modern history, every serving Latin American president—with the exception of Cuba's Fidel Castro—was democratically elected. Street protestors have toppled about half a dozen leaders since 2000, yet every change of government followed constitutional procedure. In each case—except for Ecuador and Venezuela—the military played no significant role. Latin America's democracies are far from perfect. Because public service is rife with corruption and incompetence, principled and ambitious people usually favor a career in business or academia instead of dirtying their hands in politics. But that leaves the formal reins of power in the hands of those least able to use them.

Yet the quality of politics is generally improving. The corruption scandal enveloping Brazilian President Luiz Inacio Lula da Silva did not trigger mayhem. A congressional investigation fingered several of his closest aides who were expelled from Congress, probably ending their political careers and possibly obliterating the ruling Workers Party in this year's [2006] elections. Politicians are still beholden to big business—and the unions—that finance their campaigns. But regular and clean elections are forcing them to respond to voters interests, a revolutionary development. Tax evasion is receding slowly, strengthening the concept of voters holding governments accountable—although this is a word that still does not exist in Spanish or Portuguese.

Economic Reform

A decade of economic reform is transforming the region. Credit is the lifeblood of modern economies and lending is expanding at breathtaking speed. Latin America is still relatively unbanked, but mortgages, personal loans, auto finance and credit cards that were once only for the rich, are now available to anyone with some kind of income. At a broader macroeconomic level, deregulation is fostering more competition, which creates innovation, jobs and wealth. Trade barriers have fallen, opening Latin America to the benefits of global trade and the magic of [nineteenth-century British economist] David Ricardo's theory of comparative advantage. Total trade rose from $750 billion in 2000 to over $1 trillion in 2005. Competition is making big companies become more entrepreneurial and imaginative—just look at Mexico's Cemex. Unfortunately, these companies are still rare.

Although a lot of Latin Americans vilify the 'neo-liberal agenda' and all it stands for, 13 million people escaped poverty in Latin America in the last three years [2002–2005]. That still leaves 40% of the region's population—213 million people—struggling with poverty. Although 88 million of the poor are indigents, progress in poverty reduction is undeniable.

Democratically elected governments focus less on big-ticket white elephant projects beloved of the authoritarian regimes of [the] 1970s and more on the needs of people. Governments are mobilizing enormous resources to tackle basic health and education. Brazil spends 6% of its GDP [gross domestic product] on education. Latin America has achieved universal first grade enrollment, and secondary school enrollment has more than doubled since 1990, when less than one-third of children stayed in school. In Brazil, the proportion of university students has doubled to nearly half the college-age population. Literate, better-educated and healthier people become better, more successful citizens and less likely to be bamboozled by old-style politicians whose stock in trade is paternalism and election-rigging.

Resistance from the Elites

Naturally, everything is relative. Latin America may be heading in the right direction but it's moving too slowly. It's just not growing fast enough to meet the needs of its people or keep up with progress elsewhere in the world.

Democracy Is Alive in Latin America

From all available indications, democracy, understood as the pursuit of an open and competitive system of governance based on rules accepted by all, is more alive in the hemisphere than in any other period in its history. Even in the Venezuela of President Hugo Chavez, who has obvious caudillistic inclinations, the press has remained quite open and free, although under constant pressure. The power monopoly once held by Mexico's Institutional Revolutionary Party (PRI) is part of history. In Brazil, the largest and most unequal country in the region, a man of the people has led a stable government for the past two years as head of a political party built from the bottom up. Economic calamity did not make Argentineans turn their back on democracy, as one could expect given the country's turbulent history.

Paulo Sotero,
"Democracy in Latin America: Alive but Not Well,"
Foreign Policy, *January/February 2005.*

I think that this is due less to reform fatigue and more to resistance by elites who realize how free trade, smaller governments (and the accompanying loss of state subsidies and favors), more effective tax collection and greater deregulation upset the status quo. The ineptitude of Mexico's antitrust authorities is all the more extraordinary when one considers that a few powerful groups control almost every sector of the economy—telecoms, banking, television, brewing, cement and retail. The same applies across the region. Latin America has 1,039 listed companies worth over $1 trillion. But nearly all are closely held groups controlled either by the state, a single individual or descendants of their founder. Popular capitalism does not exist in Latin America.

In the 1990s, Latin America amazed the world with daring macroeconomic reforms that crushed inflation, privatized hundreds of companies and pulled in hundreds of billions of dollars in foreign investment. Latin America's old-fashioned leftists bitterly criticized these policies—and still do, of course—but most governments were in fact too timid. None dared to completely recast their economies to improve the quality of public spending or revamp tax codes to lower marginal rates and broaden the tax base. Few countries truly liberalized their trade regimes, deregulated domestic markets to abolish barriers to entry or provided secure property rights—initiatives included in the Washington Consensus. It's depressing that the insights of [Peruvian economist] Hernando de Soto, admired and respected around the world, have made so little impact in Latin America.

The predictable result of this half-baked approach—worsened by a hostile global economic environment—was economic stagnation, indebtedness and growing contempt for economic rationality. Latin America is doing better now of course, but it could do a lot better if it learned from the experiences of others. It's sad that pro-market policies are so closely identified with the detested administration of US President George W. Bush and (erroneously) with the interests of local establishments. Argentina's Nestor Kirchner or Hugo Chavez in Venezuela—like Castro—are so popular because they have stood up to the US, the International Monetary Fund and business groups, even though their policies are ultimately self-destructive.

Chile's Example

We know from experience which economic policies work. Chile is justly celebrated for its successful market-driven economy, expertly managed by leftists who embrace the ideas enshrined in the Washington Consensus. Generations of great economists—from Adam Smith and David Ricardo to Milton Friedman and Jagdish Bhagwati—have explained how free markets and free trade bring growth and prosperity. Unfortunately, these powerful ideas have a weak hold in Latin America beyond Chile's borders.

Latin Americans also see globalization as a mortal threat because the region lacks the self-confidence to compete. Instead of realizing how participation in the global marketplace can raise living standards—the idea behind the theory of comparative advantage—people believe trade impoverishes. Defeatism encourages people to give up and emigrate. Today, Latin America's most lucrative exports are its own people, who this year will send $50 billion home in worker remittances.

Imagine how revolutionary the full application of democracy and market economics—the mantra of the 1990s—would be. I am convinced that the greatest beneficiaries of the neoliberal agenda are the poor and middle classes, not big business. Protectionism, subsidies and bureaucracy benefit oligarchs, not entrepreneurs. Enforcing public accountability of governments might even lead to an assault on bureaucracy, curbing corruption and delivering high-quality public services and an efficient judiciary. The result would be a huge acceleration in growth and welfare. Radical free-market policies could double growth rates and eliminate poverty within our lifetimes.

If not, feeble growth and continued poverty will enable populists to keep setting the agenda as they are in this election year. It really would be too bad if new leaders elected in 2006 decided to slow down or give up on reform altogether. That really would condemn Latin America to poverty and marginalization for generations.

| "*Populism is a real threat to freedom in Latin America today. It can be seen as a distortion of democracy.*"

Populism in Latin America Poses a Threat to Democracy

Fernando Henrique Cardoso

In the following viewpoint, Fernando Henrique Cardoso contends that populism in Latin America is not a mere shift to the left but a rejection of democratic principles. In a democracy, he asserts, policy is determined by laws and institutions; populist policy, on the other hand, is based on personality and personal ambition. Moreover, Cardoso claims, because populists identify themselves as outside the political establishment, they can justify silencing opposition and acting outside the law. Another danger is that populists gain their popularity through empty rhetoric rather than informed opinion, he concludes. Cardoso was Brazil's president from 1995 to 2002.

As you read, consider the following questions:

1. What happened in Latin America during the 1980s and 1990s, in Cardoso's view?

Fernando Henrique Cardoso, "More Than Ideology: The Conflation of Populism with the Left in Latin America," *Harvard International Review*, Summer 2006. Reproduced by permission.

2. According to the author, where does the legitimacy of a democracy rest and to what extent is it conferred?

3. In the author's opinion, what is still needed to consolidate democracy for good in Latin America?

If one reads current press reports and academic analyses on Latin America, the prevailing opinion seems to be that the left is making a comeback. Even though there is some truth to this perception, the political changes that are occurring in Latin America are much more complex than simply a general shift toward the political left. Oversimplication obscures rather than clarifies the current movements in Latin America. Circumstances within individual countries have resulted not in a common response but in a broad array of national responses to current challenges. In my view, the general movement toward the left in Latin America does not represent a change in ideology; instead, it represents a sentiment of dissatisfaction among voters caused by insufficient economic growth and the systematic failure of traditional institutions of representative democracy to ensure a higher standard of living for everyone.

Decades of Accelerated Change

The 1980s and 1990s were a period of deep and accelerated change in Latin America. Political and economic reforms were implemented simultaneously. Democracy replaced military rule and was portrayed as more than simply an improved political architecture. It was also supposed to bring economic prosperity, thereby providing a powerful justification for new leaders to advance the cause of democracy. Economically, Latin America was largely stagnant in the late 1980s. Because of the relative success of inward-oriented models in the 1960s and 1970s, most Latin American countries maintained some of these policies well beyond their usefulness and were late in adopting open policies. Hand in hand with democratization was thus the need for Latin American nations to succeed in economic matters. Few people realized the dangers of blending the pains of globalization with the merits of democracy. Furthermore, expectations were so high that they could have never been fully met. Hence, democracy became a scapegoat for the lack of economic progress in Latin America.

By the turn of the century, almost all Latin American countries had implemented a vast agenda for reform that included the opening of their economies to foreign trade, privatization, and fiscal adjustment. Many saw these first-generation reforms and the reorientation of state actions as either an ideologically motivated search for a minimal state, inspired by "neo-liberalism," or as a foreign imposition as implied by the very name of the "Washington Consensus." That also helps explain the mounting anti-US rhetoric in the region. However, few countries have been able to reap the benefits of globalization as promised by the proponents of these ideologies. Globalization is not meant to be a road to a more just world; instead, it should be justified on economic rationale alone. It is allegedly a more efficient system for allocating means of production worldwide. Those with the largest economies and the greatest investment in education have fared the best. Mexico, Brazil, and Chile are cases in point, having received an enormous inflow of foreign investment. Medium-sized economies such as Argentina and Colombia are at a halfway point. Smaller economies, especially in South America, have lost out with globalization. This would probably have been the case with Venezuela as well, were it not for the oil price bonanza of the past few years. Central American countries have generally fared somewhat better by negotiating preferential access to the US market for their exports.

Populism as the Common Thread

Several of the new Latin American leaders have been able to exploit the shortcomings of the past reforms. They claim leftist credentials and have a demagogic mind-set that looks back rather than forward in the content of their inflammatory, populist speech. That is not to say, however, that they belong to a single movement that is shaping the entire region. Latin America is not a uniform political landscape; there is no ideological consistency among its new leaders. It is not, therefore, that the left is making a comeback in Latin America. It would be more appropriate to say that populism is reappearing in new forms. . . .

There is more diversity than unity among Latin American leaders of the left. Most of them, however, have so far not been questioning the economic reform measures implemented by their predecessors. And in some instances, the heavily attacked orthodoxy and austerity of economic policies have been maintained or even strengthened, with the notable exception of Chávez in Venezuela.

This diversity among Latin American leaders makes it evident that the seeming shift in ideology toward the left is actually a non-partisan reaction to the partial failures of past economic policies and the unfulfilled promises of democracy. Followed by a wobbly return to democracy in the 1980s and 1990s, populism seems to be gaining ground in certain countries in the region, now bearing leftist colors rather than the traditional conservative colors.

The Dangers of Populism

Democracy so far has been formally preserved as candidates for any major elected post have been reluctant to challenge democratic principles openly. But populist leaders are now gaining enough strength to directly confront the rule of law. For this reason, populism is a real threat to freedom in Latin America today. It can be seen as a distortion of democracy, the result of a mass democracy that has gone overboard. Both populism and true democracy presuppose universal suffrage, increasingly urban societies, and extensive use of mass communications techniques. However, democracy is a rules-based

Democracy in Trouble in Latin America

[A United Nations Development Program (UNDP)] report draws some general conclusions that are helpful in analyzing Latin American democracy's crisis of legitimacy. The final message is quite simple: despite significant achievements over the last 25 years, regional democracy is in trouble. The report points out the persistent need to strengthen institutions—including legislatures, judiciaries and the police—and to deepen commitment to freedom of the press and human rights protection. It notes a growing disenchantment with elected political leaders who are not seen to be delivering the goods. It also acknowledges that poverty is worsening and that democracy has not significantly challenged the region's entrenched inequalities. But perhaps the most significant conclusion is that the economy cannot and should not be excluded from democratic decision-making.

Terry Gibbs,
"Democracy's Crisis of Legitimacy in Latin America,"
Global Policy Forum, *July 2004. www.globalpolicy.org.*

framework, a political system dependent on the smooth functioning of institutions. Institutions and rules matter more than the person who holds power. By contrast, populism tends to be shaped by the personalities, personal ambitions, and political views of those who are in command, usually a charismatic and authoritarian leader. But it may very well be the case that a group of persons also comes to exert populist leadership. The military in Brazil, for example, toyed with populism in the 1970s when the economy was growing rapidly. Legitimacy in democracies rests essentially in the results of the ballot box. It is conferred upon a democratic government only to the extent that the rule of law is applied and enforced. Populism seeks legitimacy in exactly the opposite way; it seeks legitimacy in heavy criticism of the "old political establishment" and of the complex mediation processes of representative democracy. Populist leaders define themselves as "outsiders" who have established a direct connection with the population. That justifies the fact that they can allegedly do without rules, without institutions, and without diversity of opinion. They often resort to referenda or to other forms of direct democracy, as if they were more legitimate by themselves rather than with the true mechanisms of representative democracy.

Finally, populism is based on manipulation and propaganda rather than deeds and informed opinion when it comes to making use of mass communication. Most populist leaders are good communicators, albeit with scant use of truth. They simplify reality as they see fit. Their messages are usually simple, even though they may be delivered in the format of lengthy speeches full of empty rhetoric. The probability of success is higher if the audience is poor and uneducated and therefore more inclined to accept promises of paradise. Traditionally, this has been the case in Latin America.

A Call for Continued Reform

Of course, it is not only in Latin America that populism is making progress. Populism is spreading in Eastern Europe, not to mention the heart of Europe, as recently observed in Italy. But in no other region is the extent of the threat of populism more serious than in Latin America today. That threat may become an even more worrisome reality if Peru and Mexico eventually follow the same pattern and jump on the populist bandwagon.

What, then, is still needed to consolidate democracy for good in the region? The answer is simple: reform. Latin America needs to deepen the reform process of the 1990s rather than halt it. Reform is an unfinished business in Latin America. It must go beyond economic policy and extend to areas of the state that are closely associated with the smooth operation of institutions. Latin America as a region has been only partly reformed; it maintains many archaic institutions, and its methods are old and dysfunctional. Delivery of proper public services remains inadequate. At worst, corruption is endemic, and for all practical purposes, the state simply does not exist.

The Second Wave

This second wave of reforms would address political structures, justice, public security, and political and economic integration. These reforms are the most relevant. Political reform means more efficient and more legitimate mechanisms by which people may channel their demands and voice their concerns. Political parties and elected politicians must be held more accountable for the actions they take on behalf of voters through a forum in which government officials are exposed to a dialogue with taxpayers and citizens. This will create an enlarged space for democratic deliberation, in which actors directly representing civil society will have a greater say. Reform of justice must be pursued with a view to making it more independent, faster, and more accessible. This way, governments will be better able to combat corruption, which is a chief cause for the growing lack of credibility of congresses and public institutions.

Violence is widespread in Latin America, both in towns and in the countryside. Sometimes police forces themselves assault and blackmail ordinary people. No society can survive fear. No society can believe in democracy when it feels threatened by the very authorities who are supposed to offer it protection. For these reasons, public security must also be of the utmost priority. Finally, the idea of economic and political integration must be resurrected lest it disappears for lack of progress and tangible results. Integration in Latin America used to be driven by economic considerations. It seems that political decisions are now taking precedence, representing, in my view, a risk of reversing what has already been accomplished.

The way forward will call for change in some of the most deeply rooted ways in which Latin Americans behave. Progress is likely to be slow, and frustration may ensue. But there are no other options if Latin America wants to continue to take a justified pride in its democracy. There could be few more serious enemies to democracy in Latin America than the populism and demagoguery within its borders.

> "Communism is not dead in Cuba. Nei-
> ther is it dead in Brazil, Venezuela,
> Mexico, Colombia, and the other coun-
> tries of Latin America."

Communism Is Resurging in Latin America

William F. Jasper

*In the following essay, William F. Jasper argues that Commu-
nism is thriving in Latin America. Venezuela's President Hugo
Chávez is a self-proclaimed Communist and has close ties to
Cuba's Fidel Castro, who has built a Communist network in the
region, the Sao Paulo Forum (SPF), notes Jasper. Communist
parties in Argentina, Brazil, and Chile are SPF members, as are
terrorist organizations such as the Revolutionary Armed Forces
of Colombia (FARC). If the United States fails to acknowledge
this rise of Communism, Jasper contends, it will soon find itself
surrounded by hostile regimes. Jasper is senior editor for the conservative journal* New American.

As you read, consider the following questions:

1. According to Jasper, why did Communist regimes in
   Latin America during the Cold War years fail to last?

William F. Jasper, "Communism's Resurgence: Communism Is Not Dead in Latin
America. In Fact, the Dominoes Are Falling South of the Border, but No One Seems to
Be Noticing," *New American*, vol. 21, January 24, 2005, pp. 16–20. Copyright © 2005
American Opinion Publishing Incorporated. Reproduced by permission.

2. What Communist governments and terrorist organizations outside of Latin America are guests of the SPF, according to the author?

3. In the author's view, why does the Chávez regime boast considerable prestige, revenue, and political leverage throughout Latin America?

"It's a new day. Communism is dead. It's even dead in Cuba." So declared Senator Barbara Boxer (D-Calif.) at a Senate Commerce Committee hearing in May 2002. "I hate to say it," she continued, "it's dead." The senator's proclamation was a surprise, no doubt, to Fidel Castro, whose regime was (and is) alive and as Red as ever. It also must have come as welcome news to the people of Cuba, still suffering, after nearly half a century, under Fidel's stifling oppression. Unfortunately, for them, the senator was wrong, as usual.

Conservatives had a field day blasting Senator Boxer's ridiculous epitaph. But while ridiculing her forensic pathology regarding Cuba, her critics frequently repeated Boxer's error by proclaiming that "Communism is dead" in the rest of Latin America.

Communism Is Alive

The supposed corpse of Communism, however, is very much alive. In fact, it is much more dangerously alive than it was when Castro was in his heyday, in the 1960s and '70s, sponsoring revolution and terrorism throughout the Americas, Africa, and the Middle East. Consider:

- For the past six years [since entering office in 1999], President Hugo Chavez—a self-proclaimed Communist and boon companion of Fidel—has been tightening the vise of dictatorship on Venezuela, the region's key oil-producing country (and the source of much of our imported fuel).

- Next door in Brazil, Latin America's largest, most populous nation, President Luiz Inacio Lula da Silva is also consolidating a Marxist regime.

- In Argentina, President Nestor Kirchner reversed 15 years of Argentine policy by re-establishing ties with Cuba and cozying up to Castro and Hugo Chavez.

- In Ecuador, radical Castro-Chavez protégé Lucio Gutierrez is now in control.

- Much of Colombia is controlled by FARC, the Communist narco-terrorists who have been waging a murderous terrorist war for 40 years.

- United Nations "peacekeepers" occupy Haiti, and that disaster-ridden island may soon see the return of ousted Marxist madman Jean-Bertrand Aristide.

- Riots in Bolivia caused President Lozada to resign in 2003, and the current president, Carlos Mesa, may soon be replaced by Evo Morales, "indigenous" activist and leader of the Movement Toward Socialism (MAS) party. In the December 2004 local elections, Morales' MAS candidates won many of the city and provincial races. [Morales was elected president in 2006].

- The Communist Sandinistas have swept back into power in Nicaragua, taking many of the local offices in the November 2004 elections.

The leftist list goes on: Chile's Ricardo Lagos (elected in 2000), Peru's Alejandro Toledo (2000), and Uruguay's Tabare Vazquez (2004). Latin American countries are falling like dominoes. But scarcely anyone is mentioning the Domino Theory—no, make that Domino Reality—playing out right next door.

The Domino Theory

Mention of the Domino Theory tends to draw blank stares from the under-40 set today. During the 1950s, '60s and '70s, however, it was a household word and a central tenet of U.S. and Western geo-strategy in relation to the Soviet Union, China, and the Soviet-bloc countries. If the West didn't oppose the Communist forces backed by Moscow and Beijing, the theory went, the countries of Laos, Cambodia, and Vietnam would fall to Communism, one by one, in quick succession. Millions of people would be slaughtered, and whole nations would be turned into concentration camps. The Asian nations in the region that didn't fall to overt Communist takeover would come under Red China's dominance, nonetheless.

The liberal intelligentsia sneered at such "simplistic" and "paranoid" notions. They were wrong, of course—fatally, horribly wrong. The "simplistic" theory proved to be fact. Laos, Cambodia, and Vietnam did fall like dominoes. Millions were slaughtered, and the survivors were enslaved in concentration camps. The rest of Asia has come under China's economic and military dominance.

The Latin American Difference

During the same period that the Asian dominoes were being set up for their tragic fall (the 1950s, '60s, and '70s), a similar scenario was developing much closer to home, on our southern doorstep. Fidel Castro took Cuba and used it as a revolutionary launch pad for the hemisphere. The dominoes began falling in Latin America to Soviet-backed thugs and terrorists: Romulo Betancourt in Venezuela, Cheddi Jagan in British Guiana, Juan Bosch in the Dominican Republic, Juan Jose Arevalo in Guatemala, Janio Quadros and Joao Goulart in Brazil, Victor Paz Estenssoro in Bolivia, Salvador Allende in Chile, Omar Torrijos in Panama, Maurice Bishop in Grenada, and the Sandinistas in Nicaragua.

But Communist regimes never stuck in Latin America. The major reason: geography. The Russian and Chinese Communists could not consolidate control by simply marching in massive occupying armies, like they did in Central and Eastern Europe and Central and Southeast Asia. Except for Cuba, that is, where the Kennedy administration gave Castro a security guarantee, pledging not to attempt to overthrow him, and not to allow anyone else to do so either—so long as the Russians removed their missiles. But outside of Castro's protected "workers' paradise," anti-Communist forces (often from the military) regularly toppled the Moscow-Havana puppets.

Terrorists-'R'-Us

During the 1990s, while Establishment analysts were proclaiming Communism dead in Latin America, Castro was busily building a hemispheric network that would focus on taking power by the ballot as well as the bullet. One of the most important parts of that network is the Sao Paulo Forum, a veritable Who's Who of terrorist groups and revolutionary parties that proudly boasts regular attendance by national presidents, other prominent politicians, labor leaders, and NGOs (non-governmental organizations).

The Sao Paulo Forum (SPF) was created in Sao Paulo, Brazil, in 1990, under the official sponsorship of Fidel Castro and Brazil's Communist Workers Party, headed by Lua da Silva, now president of Brazil. Member organizations of the SPF include the Communist Parties of Argentina, Brazil, Chile, Cuba, Ecuador, El Salvador, Mexico, Nicaragua, Peru, Puerto Rico, Uruguay, and Venezuela. "Former" terrorist groups that have gone political, such as Nicaragua's Sandinistas and El Salvador's FMLN, are also SPF members. So are organizations that are currently on the U.S. State Department's list of active terrorist groups, such as Colombia's FARC and ELN, the Tupac Amaru of Peru, Chile's MIR, and the Basque ETA of Spain.

The SPF conferences regularly feature guests and observers from Communist governments such as North Korea and Vietnam, as well as the Communist Party of the United States, the Palestine Liberation Organization, and Sinn Fein (the political arm of the terrorist Irish Republican Army, IRA). In short, the SPF is a global Terrorists-'R'-Us, where leaders of terrorist states and terrorist groups are allowed to vote and are given a podium from which to pontificate on human rights, justice, and democracy. Besides Cuba's Fidel Castro, SPF stalwarts include Brazil's Lula, Venezuela's Chavez, Ecuador's Gutierrez, Uruguay's Vazquez, and many other current and former government leaders. . . .

The Sao Paulo Forum

The Sao Paulo Forum is a continuation and expansion of the Tricontinental Conference, the Soviet terror operation that spawned the modern global terrorist phenomenon four decades ago. The Tricontinental made its debut appearance in 1966 with a gathering of world terrorist leaders in Havana. Although it was hosted by Fidel Castro, who became the titular head of the ongoing Tricontinental terror wave, the whole affair was completely a Moscow-run global strategic offensive. Planning for the Tricontinental had been set in motion by the Soviet Politburo at least as early as 1964, under the guidance of Boris Ponomarev, head of the Kremlin's International Department. The 1966 Havana conference brought together more than 500 representatives from Communist parties, revolutionary organizations, and terrorist groups from around the world. Cuba became the chief center of terrorist training, under the direction of Soviet KGB Colonel Vadim Kochergine and 10,000 Soviet military "advisers." Additional Communist-bloc trainers from Czechoslovakia, Bulgaria, Romania, and East Germany supplemented Cuba's massive Soviet contingent. . . .

The Sao Paulo Forum is guided by a coordinating body called the Working Group, comprised of the Communist par-

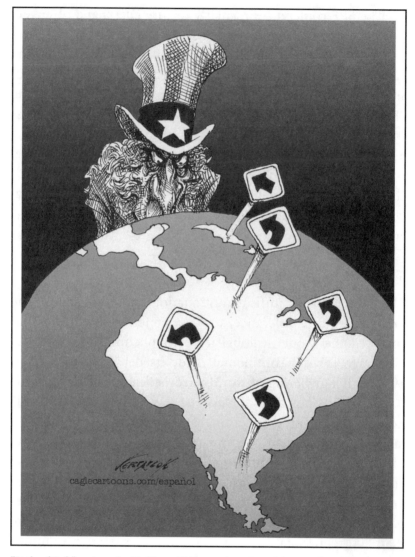

"Buds of Left," cartoon by Nerilicon, *El Economista*. Copyright 2005 by Nerilicon and CagleCartoons.com. All rights reserved.

ties of Cuba, Brazil, and Uruguay, and representatives of such terrorist groups as the FSLN, FMLN, FARC, and ELN. Like the Tricontinental, the SPF's conferences are drenched in the Marxist dialectic and replete with denunciations of "Yankee imperialism" and "savage capitalism."

Creating Many Vietnams

In 1966, at the Havana Tricontinental Conference, Castro's revolutionary sidekick, Che Guevara, called for the "creation of two, three, many Vietnams," meaning that Communists throughout the world should create multiple war fronts that would overwhelm the response capabilities of the U.S. military. Che's war cry was picked up and echoed by leftists across the globe and has remained a theme of Fidel Castro's Tricontinental/Sao Paulo Forum axis. Venezuela's Hugo Chavez is determined to implement Che's famous war cry and to carry on the Communist legacy of his aging compadre, Fidel Castro. Chavez lionizes the "martyred" Che Guevara and was interviewed in 2004 by Che's daughter, a Communist propagandist and physician who lives in Cuba.

Hugo Chavez has made a point of praising, visiting, and embracing the most totalitarian regimes in the world. He was the first head of state to visit Saddam Hussein in Iraq after the Gulf War. He has allied himself closely with Red China, Russia, Iran, Libya, Algeria, Syria, and, of course, Cuba. His administration praises the Communist regime of North Korean madman Kim Jong II—leader of an economic basket case, as well as a human rights hellhole—as a model for Venezuela's development. On October 12, 1999, during a state visit to China, President Chavez proudly announced: "I have been very Maoist all my life." He praised Mao Zedong, one of the greatest mass murderers in history, and let it be known that he viewed Chairman Mao's program as a model for his own Venezuelan revolution.

Chavez calls his program a "Bolivarian revolution," claiming inspiration from the popular 19th-century South American independence fighter Simon Bolivar. But it is clearly more Marxist and Maoist than Bolivarian. Recognizing that his hold on power was tenuous, Chavez imported thousands of Cuban agents masquerading as teachers, health professionals, scientists, and sports instructors. Their job is to organize his Bolivarian Circles—the Communist mobs patterned after Castro's Committees in Defense of the Revolution. At the same time, Chavez has brought in hundreds of intelligence agents from Castro's DGI (Cuba's version of the KGB) to help take over and purge the Venezuelan military and police of counter-revolutionary elements that pose a threat to his total consolidation of power. . . .

Oil and Revolution

Because Venezuela is blessed with the Western Hemisphere's largest proven conventional oil reserves, the Chavez regime automatically boasts considerable prestige, revenue, and political leverage, not only in Latin America but throughout the world. Chavez has been using these assets shrewdly to expand his influence in OPEC [Organization of the Petroleum Exporting Countries], the Organization of American States, the United Nations, the Group of 77 developing nations, and other forums. Chavez has been subsidizing Fidel Castro with below-market-price oil and is buying favors in the region with preferential oil prices for Argentina, Brazil, the Dominican Republic, Paraguay, Bolivia, Panama, Belize, El Salvador, and other countries. And since Venezuela consistently has been one of the top four foreign suppliers of oil to the U.S., Chavez exercises significant leverage over U.S. economic and political policies as well.

In 2004, Chavez entered into a massive military contract with Russia's Vladimir Putin, for a reported $5 billion in armaments. Chavez is buying attack and transport helicopters, MiG fighters, and other advanced weapons that will dramatically alter the military-political balance of the region.

No, Communism is not dead in Cuba. Neither is it dead in Brazil, Venezuela, Mexico, Colombia, and the other countries of Latin America. On this score, Senator Boxer and many other like-minded "experts" are, as usual, dead wrong. If we close our eyes to the Communist resurgence throughout our hemisphere and to the forces that are propelling this revival, we will soon find ourselves isolated and surrounded by nations controlled by hostile regimes.

"If one probes a bit deeper, beyond the labels, a far more complicated picture [of Latin American politics] can be discerned."

Populist Movement in Latin America Is Not a Return to Communism

Michael Shifter

In the following viewpoint, Michael Shifter claims that equating the populist movement in Latin America with Communism is misleading. The ideology that defined Cold War populism no longer applies, he maintains. For example, Shifter asserts, Chile's Michelle Bachelet embraces the free market, and the finance ministers of Brazil, Uruguay, and Argentina exercise the same fiscal discipline of centrist or even rightist governments. The growth of populism reflects a pragmatic response to needs of the Latin American people, not a shift toward Communism, he suggests. Shifter is vice president for policy at Inter-American Dialogue and teaches Latin American politics at Georgetown University.

Michael Shifter, "A New Politics for Latin America?" *America*, vol. 195, December 18, 2006, pp. 14–17. Copyright © 2006. www.americamagazine.org. All rights reserved. Reproduced by permission of America Press. For subscription information, visit www.americamagazine.org.

As you read, consider the following questions:

1. During what period, in Shifter's view, was the rise of populism in Latin America characterised as a "red" and "pink tide"?
2. Why is it sometimes difficult to distinguish differences between Brazil's former president, Fernando Henrique Cardoso, and its current one, Luiz Inácio Lula da Silva, according to the author?
3. In the author's opinion, why do new Latin American leaders not use the language of Venezuela's president Hugo Chávez?

It is tempting to view the string of election results in Latin America over the past year [2006] as proof that the world's most unequal region has moved to the left. Media accounts highlight the repudiation of free market-oriented policies, those widely referred to as "neoliberal" reforms and delineated in the Washington consensus of the early 1990's. Such reports also focus on the growing clamor for governments to be more committed to redressing social injustice and empowering the poor, who in most countries constitute at least half the population. Observers who see a sharp, radical turn describe a "red tide," whereas others refer to a more diluted version or a "pink tide."

A Radical, Red Tide?

Such characterizations were especially popular in early 2006, when Evo Morales was sworn in as the president of Bolivia. Morales was elected with a surprisingly strong mandate, boosted by his support from Bolivia's coca growers and, as an Aymara, the country's majority indigenous population. The traditional political establishment had failed to deliver tangible results for the poor and was discredited. Morales favored nationalization of Bolivia's natural gas industry, the second largest in Latin America after Venezuela's, a new constitution emphasizing indigenous rights, a redistribution of land and a drug policy that allows traditional uses of coca but not the processed and pernicious cocaine. Talk of a leftist resurgence was reinforced by Morales's unabashedly close alliance with Cuba's Fidel Castro, Latin America's revolutionary icon. Morales also has a very public and friendly relationship with Venezuela's Hugo Chávez, who, since becoming president in February 1999, has made uplifting the poor and defying the United States the driving forces behind his "Bolivarian Revolution."

Further evidence of a red tide and an expanding anti-United States bloc in Latin America came with the November 2006 election and remarkable comeback of Daniel Ortega, who led Nicaragua's revolutionary Sandinista government in the 1980's. On the region's political scorecard, Ortega joined Castro, Chávez and Morales in the radical column. But for most analysts, the red tide coexisted with a pink wave. The leftist surge also encompassed a competing, more moderate, pragmatic brand of social democratic politics that has been gaining ground. The tendency is best exemplified by Michele Bachelet, Chile's Socialist president who assumed office in March 2006, and Luiz Inácio da Silva, known as Lula, the president of Brazil's Workers Party, who was overwhelmingly elected to a second four-year term in October 2006. Other new leaders who fall in this category are Uruguay's Tabare Vásquez, the first leftist president in the country's history, and Alan García of Peru's APRA party, who was considerd a leftist in his first term, from 1985 to 1990.

Looking Beyond Labels

Yet if one probes a bit deeper, beyond the labels, a far more complicated picture can be discerned. True, political parties and figures associated with the traditional cold war left and with concern for greater social equality are now heading a number of Latin American governments. But what does that mean for the region in terms of actual policy content? Why are electorates voting for these parties, and which policies are such governments pursuing? The complex realities of the region will shape the answers. The ideological orientations that defined these parties during the days of the cold war have now faded, rendering a term like "left" an artificial construct.

The Socialist-led government of Bachelet, for example, and the successful administration of Ricardo Lagos before it have fully embraced the market as an engine for economic and social development and pursued friendly relations with the United States, including a free trade agreement in December 2003. Through a more competent state government pursuing an effective set of social policies in education and health, successive Chilean governments have managed to reduce the poverty level from 42 percent in 1992 to roughly 14 percent in 2005. Chile has had sound economic management and been rewarded with impressive economic performance. Much of this success can be attributed to the adoption of the economic reforms associated with the widely criticized Washington consensus.

Lula da Silva, too, has presided over a Workers Party government in Brazil that demonstrates noteworthy fiscal discipline. Though his re-election was largely a result of income-transfer social programs (*bolsa familiar*) for the poor and Lula's own personal charisma, his government has undoubtedly been friendly to the market. The prospect of another four-year term was welcomed by Washington and financial markets, including Wall Street. One wonders why Lula is regarded as a leftist political leader, while his predecessor, Fernando Henrique Cardoso, was considered a center-right president. Lula has essentially continued and built on the key measures implemented during Cardoso's two terms in office. In the realm of economic and social policies at least, it is hard to identify dramatic differences. Still, Lula is seen as leftist and Cardoso as center-right. This stems largely from the history of

Obscuring Gradations of Policy

Any relevant analysis of the "New Left" must take as a given that the characteristics of each country are specific if not unique. The mistake of taking such a high-visibility administration like that of Venezuela's Hugo Chavez, and using it as a benchmark for like-minded governments in the region, is made far too often; this appellation commits a disservice if it is used to obscure the political gradations of policy which distinguish one country from another and the depth of those differences. It is important to counter this overly simplistic tendency to amalgamate countries that challenge one aspect or another of the bona fides behind Washington's regional policy but nothing else. All the more so when the rest of the hemisphere is aggressively reacting to Washington's failed neo-liberal economic medications.

Larry Birns and Montana James,
"Is the 'New Left' Simply More of the Same
or a New Political Force in Latin America?"
COHA, November 26, 2007. www.coha.org.

Lula's Workers Party and his own remarkable personal story, rising up from poverty to become a hugely popular union and political leader.

Maintaining Economic Continuity

Similarly, the policy priorities of Uruguay's first "leftist" government, under Tabare Vásquez, are hard to distinguish from those of the center-right administrations that preceded it. Economic policies have been very prudent, social spending has been held in check, and the fiscal deficit is under control. In addition, Vásquez, unlike his predecessors, is currently exploring a free trade deal with the United States. The government may appear leftist at a superficial level, but invoking that term is somewhat misleading. The finance ministers in place today in such countries as Brazil, Chile, Uruguay and even Argentina, which is sometimes seen as more radical because of its defiance of the international financial system, are as orthodox as those in centrist or rightist governments.

In the same way, it is difficult to argue that the change from Alejandro Toledo to Alan García in Peru reflects a shift to the left. García's economic team, after all, is as conservative as was Toledo's. García has lavished praise on the wonders of free markets and globalization. He and his party enthusiastically embrace the free trade deal with the United States (already approved by the Peruvian Congress, but not the U.S. Congress). Most Peruvians do not care whether García's government is left, center or right, as long as it is competent and produces results (which would be a welcome contrast with his first, disastrous term).

A Different Daniel Ortega

One can even argue that the governments that form part of the red streak are not altogether left, in the traditional sense of the term. Nicaragua's Ortega, for example, is no longer the wild-eyed revolutionary of the 1980's, intent on confiscating private property. Instead, he has become a cynical, corrupt party boss, willing to make deals with anyone, even former enemies, provided they increase his own power. True, he is loyal to Castro and Chávez, but it seems almost certain that when faced with limited options for forging a viable government, Ortega will be a pragmatist.

Thus far even Bolivia's President Evo Morales has been inconsistent in defining the main policy thrusts of his government. Some of his moves, like the nationalization and military takeover of the natural gas fields on May 1, 2006, have been quite radical. But a variety of circumstances, including pressure from Brazil and other countries with a stake in Bolivia, have forced Morales to govern in more pragmatic fashion—witness his decision not to go ahead with nationalization of the mining sector. Chávez's influence in Bolivia may eventually diminish, as the Morales government explores its options and charts its own course. Bolivia, like other Latin American governments, is likely to resist unquestioned loyalty to any single ideological bloc. Rather, over time it will try to become independent, making alliances only when self-interest dictates.

Measuring Chávez as a Leader

Latin America's perceived move to the left has been closely tied to the potential influence of Chávez's Bolivarian Revolution, which has been fueled by record oil prices. Chávez is indeed Latin America's most influential leader today, not because his agenda is embraced and endorsed by other regional leaders, but because he has managed to set the terms of debate. To his credit, Chávez has put his finger on a fundamental grievance felt in Venezuela and throughout much of Latin America. It is no accident that Chávez emerged in Venezuela, the South American country that suffered two "lost decades," with its national income dropping by over 40 percent in the 1980's and 1990's. Not surprisingly, Chávez's relentless attacks on the increasingly corrupt, unresponsive and insulated traditional political order had great appeal and continue to account for part of his support today.

Still, despite an oil bonanza and weak political opposition, Chávez has not been able to devise effective solutions to Venezuela's economic problems. A charismatic communicator who thrives on conflict and confrontation, Chávez does not excel in governing—the quality Venezuelans most need and want. The social programs, or *misiones*, put in place under Chávez—for literacy training, medical services, subsidized food and the like—have helped poor Venezuelans. But the government has not put in place solutions to the problem of poverty that will be sustainable in the long term. Unemployment levels are unchanged; and common crime, which disproportionately affects the poorest in the population, has increased. Moreover, the government has exhibited autocratic, authoritarian tendencies, reflected in an unprecedented concentration of power with virtually no checks and balances. For a region that favors democracy and is striving to make it work better, the model Chávez has constructed has little appeal.

It is even a stretch to characterize what Chávez has accomplished—or failed to accomplish—as an example of "leftist" government. Ironically, notwithstanding his belligerent assaults on the [George W.] Bush administration and his indictment of globalization and free trade pacts, Chávez has extensive commercial relations with the United States, which is the market for well over half his oil exports. (Peruvians and Colombians often quip that their friendly relations with Washington do not get them the full access to U.S. markets that politically hostile Venezuela enjoys because of its oil.) Chávez's experiment—an eclectic blend of authoritarianism, populism and militarism, sustained by high oil prices—is hardly captured by the term "left."

Chávez's now infamous speech at the U.N. General Assembly in September 2006, calling President Bush the "devil," is also not a feature of the new breed of leaders in Latin America. Such language offends Latin American sensibilities and causes discomfort among other, supposedly friendly governments. It is instructive to contrast Chávez's speech with those made by Lula, Bachelet, Kirchner and even Morales at the United Nations. The language of these leaders was much more moderate and conciliatory. Still, many in Washington fail to grasp that all Latin American governments—regardless of political orientation—want more "elbow room" and distance from the United States, because their options for economic relationships have multiplied with globalization. It is less helpful to characterize this tendency as part of a shift to the "left" than as a product of global changes that challenge traditional notions of Latin America as the strategic preserve or backyard of the United States.

A Fundamental Social Agenda

Another fundamental orientation that has emerged from the current round of elections in Latin America is the growing importance of the social agenda in each country's politics. Even where more conservative candidates won, like Felipe Calderón of the PAN party in Mexico, the results were clearly an expression of widespread discontent and frustration. Andrés Manuel López Obrador, who rejected the neoliberal model of free markets and globalization and appealed to the frustration of the poor, especially in the south, nearly won the election. The results in Peru can be read in a similar way. Although García won, Ollanta Humala, the radical outsider candidate who attacked the political order and neoliberal economic model, received 48 percent of the vote, concentrated in the poorer, southern part of the country.

The electoral results in Mexico, Peru and other countries revealed tremendous popular anger and social polarization in Latin America. They should be wake-up calls for the newly elected political leadership. So far, no single model or alternative has taken hold in the region. Above all, Latin Americans want governments that combine economic growth with greater attention to the social agenda, governments that are both honest and effective. It is doubtful that using labels like left, red or pink will yield any clues as to how to heed such a popular and legitimate demand.

> "Through democracy, the poor—once
> the most disenfranchised populations
> in Latin America—have become the
> most powerful political force."

The Rise of Populism in Latin America Can Be Explained by Political Pragmatism

Jaime Daremblum

In the following viewpoint, Jaime Daremblum maintains that most of Latin America's leaders employ populist rhetoric for practical, rather than ideological, reasons. The poor gained political force as democracy grew in Latin America, he claims, and to be elected, leaders must use populist rhetoric that endorses social programs. To improve its image in Latin America, the United States should follow the lead of Latin American leaders and lend more support to the region's social programs, he concludes. Daremblum is director of the Center for Latin America Studies at the Hudson Institute, a conservative think tank.

Jaime Daremblum, "A Pragmatic Left in Latin America?" *Washington Post*, December 13, 2006. Reproduced by permission of the *Washington Post*.

As you read, consider the following questions:

1. According to Daremblum, why should American policy-makers avoid a one-size-fits-all approach to Latin America?

2. In the author's opinion, how will his hard-fought 2006 reelection as president of Venezuela change Hugo Chávez's focus?

3. Why does Nicaragua's Daniel Ortega sound more like a pragmatist than a revolutionary, in the author's view?

Not so long ago, Brazilian president Luiz Inacio "Lula" da Silva was widely considered a Castroite intent on a Communist-style centralization of Brazil's economy and the subversion of neighboring democracies. Yet after four years of surprisingly responsible governance, Lula no longer sets off alarm bells in Washington. American policymakers should keep him in mind before dismissing the new leaders of Nicaragua and Ecuador as authoritarian extremists in the same vein as Venezuelan president Hugo Chavez.

Those leaders, Daniel Ortega and Rafael Correa, are both well known men of the left. As the boss of Nicaragua's Sandinista party, Ortega spent much of the 1980s turning his country into a Soviet client state, while fighting off the U.S.-backed Contra rebels. Correa, meanwhile, is a self-described "personal friend" of Chavez who wants to fundamentally overhaul the Ecuadorian constitution.

One Size Does Not Fit All

While Mr. Chavez will likely continue his anti-American antics, there are signs that Ortega and Correa have more practical, pro-growth, pro-U.S. positions in mind.

In any event, a well reasoned, innovative and more active U.S. diplomacy towards Latin America could further reduce Chavez's ability to spread his so-called revolution to other Latin American nations. American policymakers should therefore avoid a one-size-fits-all approach to the region and opt for case-by-case decisions instead. America should also reward good governance by giving economic and social assistance to moderate Latin American leaders, a point well made ... by Costa Rican president Oscar Arias during a visit to Washington.

It is helpful to understand how leftist candidates arrived in office. These men have attracted voters most affected by minimal economic opportunities, namely the poor. Some 40 percent of Latin Americans live below the poverty line, and inequality rates remain the worst in the world: The lowest fifth of the population receives 4.5 percent of national income, while the highest fifth accounts for 55 percent, according to studies conducted by the Inter-American Development Bank (IDB). This poverty is concentrated especially in the rural population, women, and indigenous people. A quarter of poor people in Latin America are indigenous, a proportion reaching 60 percent in the Andean and Middle American countries—a huge swath of the electorate. Political turbulence therefore increases with the extent that the population is indigenous.

Through democracy, the poor—once the most disenfranchised populations in Latin America—have become the most powerful political force. Leftist leaders have been quick to endorse new programs and entitlement for the poor. Add this to the prevailing disappointment with traditional ruling elites, and the election results are no surprise. Chavez's decisive re-election on December 3, [2006], shows how heavily these factors still weigh in some Latin American nations.

The Risks of the Chavez Connection

Chavez, however, has touted this populist theme at home and abroad so much, and with so much anti-Americanism, that being too close to him is becoming a political liability. Correa, for example, was favored to win his election in the first round, but his friendship with Chavez landed him in second place. To

Looking for Different Solutions

Latin America, a region whose economies have picked up quite strongly over the past five years and is otherwise enjoying ... the benefits of the worldwide commodity boom, is still grappling with a 40-per-cent poverty rate and the highest inequality anywhere. Sick and tired of the "Washington consensus" policies that were rammed down the throats of almost all countries in the region during the 1990s, the electorates have been searching for different solutions.

Jorge Heine,
"Chavez's Loss Is a Turning Point for Latin America,"
Globe & Mail *(Toronto, Canada), December 4, 2007.*

prevail in the run-off, he had to distance himself from the Venezuelan. Earlier [in 2006] Ollanta Humala in Peru had looked like a shoo-in, but lost precisely because of the open interference of Chavez in his favor. And in this year's Mexican election, mere comparisons with Chavez by his opponent contributed to the defeat of Andres Manuel Lopez Obrador—albeit by a whisker.

Even in Venezuela Mr. Chavez now faces more challenging political circumstances, despite his overwhelming victory [in December 2006]. His opponent, Manuel Rosales, ran a strong campaign and unified the anti-Chavez voters for the first time in many years. Whether or not the official results reflect the whole reality, the undeniable fact is that Rosales forced Chavez to fight for his election, something that a few months [before the election] looked all but impossible. From now on, Chavez will have to focus more on (and direct more of his oil money to) his own country and focus less on his dreams of world leadership. Two days after being reelected, in a public statement, he echoed Raul Castro's speech on Fidel's 80th birthday, calling for negotiations with the U.S. to resolve their differences.

Inter-American Relations

Lately American diplomacy seems to have resonated in Ecuador, creating an opening for Mr. Correa to steer toward the political center. Tellingly, . . . he publicized his telephone conversation with President [George W.] Bush, as well as the visit paid to him by American Ambassador Linda Jewell and the announcement of an extension of the Andean Trade Preference Act (ATPA). Correa earned a PhD in economics from the University of Illinois in Urbana-Champaign, and knows well the importance of preferential access to the U.S. market and the invigorating impact of remittances from abroad—mostly from the U.S.—worth $2 billion a year. Since Correa's Alianza PAIS party lacks representation in the new Congress, he will have to tread carefully while trying to improve the lot of impoverished countrymen as fast as possible, which requires continued economic growth.

In Nicaragua, Ortega has devoted himself to assuring investors, both foreign and local, that he intends to respect the CAFTA [Central America] free trade agreement with the U.S. and to follow responsible economic policies. He has also made public his desire to develop a good working relationship with the U.S. Scalded by the 16 years he was kept out of power due to the ruinous policies of his radical past, he sounds more like a pragmatist—or an opportunist—than a revolutionary.

Under pressure from the high expectations of their respective constituencies, the new administrations in Ecuador and Nicaragua can be expected to promote social projects aimed at fighting poverty and diminishing political instability. Like Lula in Brazil, Ortega and Correa will probably keep up some of the rhetoric of international anti-imperialism, but without becoming part of a serious bloc inimical to the United States.

We have reached a stage in Inter-American relations where the U.S. should apply more finesse when dealing with the new pragmatic left of the region. More engagement, more cooperation and more support to Latin American programs for the poor such as education and health care, and a minimum of lecturing and posturing, will make radical populism less tempting for the two newly elected leaders.

| "The Washington consensus [cutting social spending, privatizing national industries, deregulating markets, and weakening unions in Latin America] ... proved an absolute disaster."

The Rise of Populism in Latin America Is a Response to Failed U.S. Policies

Greg Grandin

In the following viewpoint, Greg Grandin argues that the populist movement in Latin America is a response to failed economic policies imposed by the United States. In return for financial support, the United States forced Latin American nations to cut social spending, privatize national industries, and eliminate trade barriers, Grandin maintains. These policies failed to achieve promised economic success and increased social inequality, he claims. In response, Grandin asserts, populist leaders promise both economic and social reform. Grandin is a professor of history at New York University and the author of Empire's Workshop: Latin America, the United States and the Rise of the New Imperialism.

Greg Grandin, "The Uprising," *New Statesman*, vol. 135, December 4, 2006, pp. 30–32.
Copyright © 2006 New Statesman, Ltd. Reproduced by permission.

As you read, consider the following questions:

1. According to Grandin, how have those committed to a 1990s vision of globalization reacted to the 2006 elections in Latin America?

2. What happened to a Latin American country that tried to break out of the U.S.-imposed provincial system during the Cold War, according to the author?

3. In the author's view, how has financial independence converted to political freedom for Latin American governments?

As Venezuelans go to the polls [in 2006], they bring to a close not just a contest between President Hugo Chávez and his main challenger, Manuel Rosales, but a year-long, continent-wide campaign. Those sharply critical of Washington-backed economic liberalisation have been pitted against those in favour of freer trade with the United States. It's been a race to the wire, with leftists taking Bolivia, Chile, Uruguay, Nicaragua and Ecuador, and centrists and conservatives holding Colombia, Peru, Costa Rica and Mexico.

An Important Election Cycle

Those committed to a vision of globalisation as it proceeded in the 1990s—reduced tariffs, deregulation, tight money and privatisation—have worked hard to brush off the importance of this election cycle. The *Wall Street Journal* and the *Economist*, for instance, repeatedly point out, correctly, that many of Latin America's new leftists, such as Luiz Inácio Lula da Silva in Brazil or Michelle Bachelet in Chile, are fiscal moderates, and that the firebrand style of Chávez is the exception not the rule for the region's reformers.

Yet, despite policy differences, and largely independently of the outcome of specific elections, Latin America is undergoing a political and economic realignment. The White House is hoping for an upset in Venezuela, but even if the improbable happens and Chávez loses [he won the election], this will only slow, not stop, the decline of US influence in the area that used to be called its "backyard".

A Strained Relationship

During the cold war, Washington counted on Latin America to watch its back as it moved about in the world. Regional governments voted en bloc in favour of the US and against the USSR at the United Nations, while bilateral economic treaties gave US corporations and banks special preference, ratifying Latin America's status as a province of the United States within an increasingly open world. When a country tried to break out of this system, the US supported coups that installed more co-operative military regimes, with death-squad auxiliaries eliminating those who continued to dissent.

Following the demise of the Soviet Union, Washington moved away from its reliance on repressive Latin American proxies, banking instead on its ability to project its power through elections and economic pressure.

This worked throughout the 1990s, as heavily indebted countries governed by centrists, grasping for the carrot of foreign investment, submitted to the command of the IMF [International Monetary Fund]. Ever mindful of the punishing stick of currency-market selloffs, they cut back social spending, privatised national industries, weakened the power of organised labour, deregulated the financial sector, and did away with trade barriers that protected local manufacturers and peasant producers.

Over the past few years, however—roughly since Chávez's landslide victory in 1998—the system has begun to break down. The Washington consensus, as this set of policies came to be called, proved an absolute disaster.

Between 1980 and 2000, the region grew cumulatively by only 9 per cent in per capita terms. Compare that with the 82 per cent expansion of the previous two decades, and add to it

A Diverse Movement

The recent upsurge of populism in the region comes as a direct riposte to Washington Consensus dogma. The populist regimes now in power in Latin America—Nicaragua, Argentina, Bolivia, Ecuador, Venezuela, Chile, and Brazil—are diverse and have varying bases of support. The rural *campesinos* and urban laborers who account for the core of Evo Morales's support in Bolivia differ demographically from the base behind the successful campaign of Rafael Correa in Ecuador. But all of these leaders are motivated by a desire for government to be results-oriented and as close as possible in policy and spirit to the aspirations of the governed.

Larry Birns and Nicholas Birns, "Hemispheric Echoes:
The Reverberations of Latin American Populism,"
Harvard International Review, *December 2007.*

the financial crises that have rolled across Mexico, Brazil, Venezuela, Bolivia, Ecuador and Argentina over the past 15 years, sweeping away accumulated savings, destroying the middle class, and wrecking the agricultural sector, and you will get a sense of why voters have turned left.

Moving Beyond Free Trade

Efforts to move beyond free-trade orthodoxy have been aided by the significant stores of capital that have been built up in Asia, Europe and the Middle East, which have helped wean Latin America off its dependence on US finance. Likewise, high oil prices have transformed Venezuela into a regional creditor, with Caracas investing its petrodollars not in US banks but in infrastructure and bonds that help neighbouring countries break free from the IMF.

When, in 2004, the Argentinian president, Néstor Kirchner, offered the holders of his country's $170bn [billion] external debt 30 cents per dollar, many predicted the markets would punish Argentina by withholding future investment. But, with Chinese capital pouring in, and Kirchner's economic prudence proving a profitable bet, such threats are not as persuasive as they once were. Similar access to alternative sources of investment has allowed not just the leftist governments of Bolivia and Venezuela, but even a conservative one in Ecuador, to negotiate more favourable contracts with multinational energy companies.

Co-operation among the region's economies is also providing Latin America with leverage. Earlier this year, the Montevideo-based Latin American Integration Association reported that trade among its 12 member nations had grown 110 per cent since 2003, a much faster pace than had been predicted. In addition, rapidly expanding trade with Europe and Asia, particularly China, has helped the region gain considerable autonomy from US markets.

With financial independence comes political freedom. Over the past couple of years, governments from across the political spectrum have demonstrated a steadfast unwillingness to enlist in Washington's "war on terror". They have rejected the Pentagon's efforts to subordinate their militaries to US command; opposed the invasion of Iraq; refused to elect the US-backed candidate to the leadership of the Organisation of American States (OAS); declined to pass a law that would have exempted the US from the International Criminal Court; and rebuffed calls to isolate Venezuela. Such dissent was unthinkable during the cold war.

A Simplistic Split

In response to this independence movement, the White House has tried to sell the idea that there are "two lefts" in Latin America: a responsible one it is willing to work with and an irresponsible one that is a threat to democracy. It gets help from commentators such as Jorge Castañeda, who divides Latin America between bad populists and good reformers, and Álvaro Vargas Llosa, who writes about a "carnivorous" and a "vegetarian" left.

Yet such a simplistic split does not hold. For one thing, it is the supposed red-meat left that has had the most economic success. Growth in Venezuela and Argentina is off the charts, with impressive declines in poverty and unemployment, while Chile and Brazil are experiencing sluggish performance.

And the "good reformers" themselves don't buy it. Leaders from Lula, Bachelet and Morales to Kirchner and Chávez share a commitment to integration, diversification and policies that spur not just growth, but fairness. It is this common agenda that led Bachelet, responding to the [George W.] Bush administration's attempt to use her moderation to criticise Chávez, to defend Venezuela as a country working to "eradicate poverty and eliminate inequality". It is also what led Lula to make his first post-re-election trip abroad to Caracas, where he announced his support for Chávez's third-term campaign.

There are real conflicts among Latin American nations that Washington could exploit: between Bolivia and Brazil over energy issues, say, or Argentina and Uruguay over trade. It is having a hard time, however, backing up its divide-and-rule strategy with real incentives. The US has tried to weaken opposition to the Free Trade Areas of the Americas by picking off low-hanging fruit such as Paraguay and Peru with bilateral economic pacts. But the Democrats, now in control of Congress, have just declared that they will block ratification of free-trade treaties with Peru and Colombia because they fail to protect labour rights. Likewise, the steady decline of the dollar has reduced the importance of the US market. So, when Washington recently threatened to revoke trade concessions to Argentina and Brazil as punishment for their resistance to regional free-trade agreements, Buenos Aires and Brasilia refused to budge.

With its political and economic influence in the region waning, the US is at a crossroads. It can either work with Latin American nationalists to develop equitable economic policies, or return to the days when it relied on repressive strongmen to enforce its authority locally. That the Pentagon [in November 2006] announced an increase in military aid to Latin America in response to the rise of the left suggests that it has already taken a step in the wrong direction.

Periodical Bibliography

The following articles have been selected to supplement the diverse views presented in this chapter.

Larry Birns and Nicholas Birns — "Hemispheric Echoes: The Reverberations of Latin American Populism," *Harvard International Review*, December 2007.

Jane Bussey — "A Struggle for Hearts and Minds," *Miami Herald*, June 26, 2006.

Duncan Currie — "Mr. Chavez's Neighborhood," *Weekly Standard*, September 24, 2007.

Richard Feinberg — "Competitiveness and Democracy," *Latin American Politics and Society*, Spring 2008.

Greg Grandin — "Latin America's New Consensus," *Nation*, May 1, 2006.

Jorge Heine — "Chavez's Loss Is a Turning Point for Latin America," *Globe & Mail (Toronto, Canada)*, December 4, 2007.

Peter Katel — "Change in Latin America," *CQ Researcher Online*, July 21, 2006.

Alvaro Vargas Llosa — "The Return of the Idiot," *Foreign Policy*, May/June 2007.

Moisés Naím — "The Good Neighbor Strategy," *Time*, July 9, 2006.

Moisés Naím — "The Lost Continent," *Foreign Policy*, November/December 2006.

Andres Oppenheimer — "In Latin America, It's the Left Versus the Left," *Miami Herald*, May 7, 2006.

Paulo Sotero — "Democracy in Latin America: Alive but Not Well," *Foreign Policy*, January/February 2005.

CHAPTER 3

What Role Should the United States Play in Latin America?

Chapter Preface

When in the nineteenth century the nations of Latin America freed themselves from Spanish and Portuguese colonial rule, the United States became the driving political and economic force in the region. However, the relationship between the United States and Latin America has often been fraught with friction. According to journalist Peter Katel, "anti-U.S. feeling is part of the political landscape in Latin America, where the region's 800-pound gorilla has been asserting dominance for nearly two centuries." U.S. influence in Latin America was primarily economic before and during World War II. In the years following, however, Latin America became a Cold War battleground. While the United States praised democratic reform, it backed repressive regimes in the region to counter left-leaning political movements with ties to Communism.

As the Soviet Union began to collapse, so did Latin American military regimes, and democracy began to spread in the region. At the same time, the United States began pushing its neoliberal economic polices. Global lenders such as the International Monetary Fund made loans to the region contingent upon the liberalization of trade and finance and privatization of publicly owned companies. In the eyes of many, the failure of these economic policies led to the rise of populist Latin American leaders in the new millennium. Indeed, these leaders often blame the United States for the region's problems, in what some see as a resurgence of anti-Americanism, which in turn colors the debate over the role the United States should play in Latin American affairs.

Some analysts assert that growing anti-American sentiment in Latin America poses a threat to the region's relationship with the United States. In their eyes, the Marxist rhetoric of Venezuela's populist President Hugo Chávez, for example, reflects a rejection of U.S. involvement in Latin America. Chávez advocates socialism and condemns imperialism, blaming the United States for the region's problems. However, U.S. policies alone do not explain Latin America's struggles, these analysts argue. The anti-American rhetoric of populist leaders does not address the role that the ruling classes have played in the region's troubles. Indeed, argues Bolivian writer Juan Claudio Lechín, "Our elites have devoted themselves simply to making money, shrugging off their responsibilities for what the people are demanding."

Other commentators claim, however, that anti-American protests do not reflect Latin American attitudes toward the people of the United States in general. They are instead a rejection of the policies of the George W. Bush administration. According to Michael Shifter of Inter-American Dialogue, "There's a special dislike and distrust for the [interventionist] policies of the Bush administration." In Shifter's view, people in Latin America still have vivid memories of Latin America's dirty wars, in which the United States played a central role. In dirty wars, the secret police or the military use kidnapping, torture, and murder against revolutionary insurgents, and civilians are often the victims. During the late 1970s, for example, thousands of people were killed or disappeared in Argentina. Like-minded commentators also note that populist leaders such as Chávez are anti-Bush, not anti-American. "Chavez and others in government are always careful to differentiate between the American people and problems they have with the Bush administration," maintains Alexander Main, an adviser to Venezuela's foreign ministry. "The long-term goal," claims Main, "is to keep strong relations with the U.S., with the hope that another administration will have more reasonable policies towards Venezuela and the rest of the world."

Whether U.S. policies toward Latin America and the rest of the world will change during the new administration of Barack Obama remains to be seen. In the meantime, commentators continue to contest whether Latin American sentiments toward the United States influence the U.S. role in the region. The authors in the following chapter debate other issues concerning the appropriate role for the United States in Latin America.

> *"The United States has already negoti-*
> *ated free trade with nine countries . . .*
> *that account for the bulk of our two-*
> *way trade in the Western Hemisphere."*

The United States Should Promote Free Trade Agreements with Latin America

Daniel Griswold

In the following viewpoint, Daniel Griswold argues that the United States should continue to encourage Latin American nations to embrace free trade. Latin American nations that have negotiated free trade agreements with the United States enjoy the benefits of the global economy, he maintains. Though populist leaders in Latin America who oppose such agreements claim that they are strengthening their nations' independence, Griswold asserts, in reality they are hurting their citizens by isolating them from the global marketplace. Griswold is director of the Center for Trade Policy Studies at the Cato Institute.

Daniel Griswold, "Our New Coalition of the Willing," Center for Trade Policy Studies, Cato Institute, February 15, 2006. www.freetrade.org. Republished with permission of Cato Institute, conveyed through Copyright Clearance Center, Inc.

As you read, consider the following questions:

1. What is the result of Latin America's political move to the left, in the author's opinion?
2. According to Griswold, where does the economic model that views trade liberalization with suspicion look for its "center of gravity"?
3. In the author's view, how important is the Free Trade Area of Americas (FTAA) agreement to the United States?

B olivia's new president, the socialist coca grower Evo Morales, promised in his inaugural address to turn his country sharply away from the American "neo-liberal" model of private enterprise and expanding trade. The election of Morales at first appears to be yet another sign that Latin Americans are moving en masse to the left, but in fact it only exposes a deepening regional fault line running roughly down the spine of the Andes Mountains.

Two Models

Latin American governments are pursuing two basic economic models that face in opposite directions. One model embraces free enterprise, macroeconomic stability, and growing engagement with the global economy, including free trade with the United States. Chile, Mexico, and El Salvador are the leading practitioners, with steady growth, rising foreign investment, and political stability as the tangible rewards.

The other model looks with suspicion, if not outright hostility, on private enterprise, foreign investment, and trade liberalization. The Venezuela of Hugo Chavez and the Cuba of Fidel Castro exemplify this model; now the Bolivia of Evo Morales is its newest follower. While the first model orients itself toward the United States and the Pacific Rim for its commercial ties, the second looks inwardly to Mercosur, the customs union that includes Brazil and Argentina, for its center

The Necessity of Latin American Co-operation

This is not the time for Latin America to abandon free trade agendas. As tempting as populist policies may be, free trade does effectively integrate Latin Americans into the global economy. This makes it harder for those forces in Latin America desperate to preserve the deadening mercantilist status-quo to resist economic reform's liberating effects.

A continent without hope is a continent without a future.

Samuel Gregg, "Free Trade: Latin America's Last Hope?"
Acton Commentary, October 24, 2007. www.acton.org.

of gravity. Indeed, the trade organization is about to welcome Venezuela and Bolivia as its newest members.

In his inaugural address, Morales promised a new era of "independence" from the United States, the nationalization of oil and natural gas resources, and a greater sharing of the nation's wealth with its poor, especially his fellow indigenous citizens. He has vowed to become a "nightmare" for Washington. The real nightmare will more likely be for the people of Bolivia.

The ditch along the road of Latin American development is littered with the wreckage of populist movements, dating back to Argentina's Juan Peron, that have tried to lift the lot of the masses by isolating their economies and redistributing income internally. Bolivia, like Venezuela, may be able to run for a while on the fumes of its energy resources, but without a vibrant, competitive, and expanding private sector, its people will continue to suffer in poverty.

The End of a Worthy Vision

For the United States, the growing ideological rift in Latin America probably spells the end of any hopes for a Free Trade Area of Americas (FTAA) within the next decade. The worthy vision of a free trade area encompassing all 34 of the more or less democratic countries in the hemisphere (all but Cuba) will be impractical as long as even a small group of governments remain essentially hostile to the principles of free trade and free markets.

Chavez, Morales, Castro, and their ideological soul-mates in the region will hail this gridlock as a rebuke against "American imperialism," when in fact the economic interest of the United States in the FTAA is small and waning. With the enactment of the Central American Free Trade Agreement, following NAFTA [North American Free Trade Agreement] and the U.S.-Chile FTA, the United States has already negotiated free trade with nine countries (including Canada) that account for the bulk of our two-way trade in the Western Hemisphere.

In fact, if the United States successfully concludes ongoing FTA talks with Panama and the Andean countries of Colombia, Ecuador, and Peru, it will have achieved FTAA-style free trade with countries that already account for 88 percent of our two-way trade. At this point, concluding an FTAA would be merely a mopping-up operation for the United States. The main beneficiaries of an FTAA would be the countries of Latin America, primarily because they would achieve free trade with each other by lowering their own barriers to trade.

A Complicated Reality

Of course, the reality in Latin America is far more complicated than any neat, bi-polar world. The leftist Prime Minister of Brazil, Luiz Inacio Lula da Silva, has governed pragmatically, pursuing orthodox macroeconomic policies while playing a constructive role in global trade negotiations. Meanwhile, some of the governments engaged in trade negotiations with the United States have proven to be reluctant partners.

The result of America's piecemeal approach to hemispheric trade negotiations has been to assemble a coalition of the more-or-less willing. Within a couple of years, this approach will unite all the Pacific Coast countries of North and South America together in free trade with the United States, if not among themselves.

No Latin American country will be forced to give up its independence, but only to choose between two paths of development: one facing outward to the world and confidently to the future, the other facing inward and fearfully to the failed policies of the past.

> "... Latin Americans, having had a bad experience with 'liberalization' of markets over the past two decades, are strongly against the kinds of radical free market policies that FTAA would impose."

Current U.S.-Latin American Free Trade Agreements Are Inequitable

David Moberg

In the following viewpoint, David Moberg claims that trade agreements with the United States have had a detrimental impact on the people and economies of Latin American nations. According to Moberg, Latin American countries are at a disadvantage from American "trade barriers and agricultural subsidies." Predictions of significant economic growth in Latin America have "led to the implementation of bad policies that in turn have increased unemployment and have left Latin Americans once again drowning in debt." Popular uprisings have led to the establishment of governments critical of FTAA, such as Brazil, Argentina, and Venezuela. Brazil, in particular, wants the

David Moberg, "Resisting Globalization: The South American Consensus on the FTAA," *In These Times*, November 10, 2003, pp. 1-2. Copyright © 2003 *In These Times*. Reproduced by permission.

United States to discuss "its procedures to fight dumping or agricultural subsidies" before it in turn will discuss the U.S. request for "deregulation of services or investor protections." David Moberg is a senior editor of In These Times. *He has also received fellowships from the John D. and Catherine T. MacArthur Foundation and the Nation Institute for research on the new global economy.*

As you read, consider the following questions:

1. According to Moberg, what do Latin Americans fear that free trade in all services will bring?
2. According to Moberg, what are the characteristics of the "Washington Consensus" model for economic development.
3. What does the example of Mexico show about the effect of free trade on a Latin American economy?

The United States is having trouble selling the latest model of souped-up global trade deals as a cure-all for the world's economic ills. First, talks in Cancun last September to expand the World Trade Organization collapsed. Now talks scheduled in Miami for November 17-21 to create a new free trade agreement for the Western Hemisphere likely will be marked by conflict and similarly end in stalemate.

One conflict will be between the Bush administration and demonstrators, who oppose the Free Trade Agreement of the Americas (FTAA) and hope to mount the largest U.S. protest against corporate globalization since the terrorist attacks of September 11, 2001, dampened a growing popular movement.

But the trade ministers will not be able to blame the protestors alone for their likely failure in negotiating the FTAA. Opposition in Latin America is widespread; hemispheric governments disagree over what should be in the agreement, and more and more economists are recognizing that the model for economic development embodied in FTAA is deeply flawed.

Negotiators had planned to wrap up talks on this new agreement, which the United States hopes will be modeled on the North American Free Trade Agreement (NAFTA), by the end of 2004. But Brazil and the United States, the negotiation co-chairs, are deeply divided. Several Latin American countries want to slow down negotiations or set aside touchy issues the United States is pushing—like expanded rights for investors—until the United States is willing to remove trade barriers and agricultural subsidies that give U.S. exports an unfair advantage. The United States also is insisting that FTAA go beyond NAFTA and deregulate all services. Countries would then have to negotiate to exclude any service they did not want deregulated. Latin Americans fear that free trade in all services could lead to the privatization of telecommunications, water delivery and even education.

Equally important, Latin Americans, having had a bad experience with "liberalization" of markets over the past two decades, are strongly against the kinds of radical free market policies that FTAA would impose.

Negotiators Face Sticking Points

Domestic politics in individual countries also will complicate discussions. With a presidential election a year away, the Bush administration is unwilling to talk about a key issue for Brazil: the high tariffs protecting the Florida citrus industry from Brazilian competition. And most of the Democratic presidential contenders are critical to varying degrees of trade strategies like FTAA, even though it was launched under Bill Clinton. Very little in the preliminary FTAA text protects worker rights and the environment, a minimal demand of most candidates. The United States is likely to propose that countries agree to enforce their own laws, but AFL-CIO trade expert Thea Lee argues that such a provision would have less influence with traditional labor rights violators, like Central American countries, than existing labor rights protections in the

U.S. trade law, which requires countries to live up to core international standards to qualify for special tariff reductions.

Neoliberal policies, including NAFTA, have not worked well for most of Latin America since they began to be imposed or adopted during the "lost" decade of the '80s. During that time Latin American countries, saddled with a massive foreign debt, averaged annual economic decline of eight-tenths of a percent per year, compared with average growth of 2.9 percent a year from 1960 to 1980. And starting in 1990, a boom decade in the United States, Latin American economies grew only an average of 1.6 percent a year. During even that period of growth, inequality and poverty in Latin America remained extremely high or got worse.

In a recent poll, only 16 percent of a broad cross-section of Latin Americans expressed satisfaction with the free market model. According to the *Financial Times*, "Most Latin Americans live in fear of losing their jobs and believe the free market reforms of the past decade have done little to improve their living standards."

Bolivians Defend Resources

In one of the most dramatic recent expressions of that sentiment, Bolivians blockaded roads and staged mass protests, bringing down neoliberal President Gonzalo Sanchez de Lozada on October 21. The protests were triggered by plans of President "Goni" to sell U.S. corporations natural gas via a new pipeline through Chile. But Bolivian peasants and miners know from centuries of experience that exports of their country's natural resources have benefited only the wealthy elite—like Goni. And they understand that since the mid-'80s when Goni was an architect of radical free market, or neoliberal, policies, inequality has increased and most Bolivians were worse off than before.

Cheap agricultural imports have since driven many peasants off the land and into urban settlements like El Alto, the

The Risks of Free Trade

As different outcomes across the region illustrate, Latin American countries often lack the essential institutions necessary to equally and fairly distribute the promised benefits of U.S.-backed FTAs [Free Trade Agreements]. . . .

Democracy in Latin America is too institutionally weak and non-inclusive to afford room for any further mishaps. Despite the indignant outcries of free traders, the absence of sufficient governmental regulations could prove highly damaging for Latin American economies, only prolonging their normally hapless struggle to reduce poverty and attain long-term stability.

Manuel Trujillo,
"Peru, Yes; Columbia? Free Trade Agreements:
Lessons from Latin America's Recent Past,"
Council on Hemispheric Affairs, December 6, 2007. www.coha.org.

center of the most militant clashes with security forces. Peasants also were incensed at the Bolivian government's enforcement of an anti-free market plan by the United States to eradicate coca, a traditional Andean crop that provided much-needed cash.

Washington Consensus Crumbles

In recent years, popular uprisings against neoliberalism have led to new governments in Brazil, Argentina and Venezuela—the countries that are now the greatest FTAA skeptics. Massive popular protests also have shaken Ecuador, Peru, Costa Rica, Colombia and Mexico. The governments in Uruguay, Paraguay and the Caribbean also have resisted much of the U.S. agenda. All governments in Latin America, even those most solicitous of the United States, know they are negotiating the FTAA with a loaded and angry popular movement cocked at their political heads.

The International Monetary Fund (IMF) has greatly misjudged the effectiveness of the "Washington Consensus" model for development, which emphasizes export-led growth, open markets, deregulation, privatization and fiscal austerity. In 13 of the last 17 years, the IMF has overestimated growth in Latin America for the coming year by an average of 1.6 percent, according to Dean Baker and David Rosnick of the Washington-based Center for Economic and Policy Research.

The rosy projections also have led to the implementation of bad policies that in turn have increased unemployment and have left Latin Americans once again drowning in debt.

The principles of the Washington Consensus are not a useful guide to promote economic growth in Latin America, Harvard University economics professor and trade expert Dani Rodrik told the World Bank last March. "The periods of economic growth have no relation with the policies of integration to the world economy."

Trade Talks Hinder Growth

Trade negotiations have been oversold as a way for countries to develop, Rubens Ricupero, secretary-general of the United Nations' Conference on Trade and Development (UNCTAD), said in October. According to UNCTAD's annual report, Latin American policies that focused on free markets and "getting prices right" blocked technological change and capital accumulation needed for growth. Former World Bank chief economist Joseph Stiglitz argues that getting institutions right, which includes greater democracy and unionization of workers, is at least as important to make trade work. Further, developing countries should grow by increasing domestic demand through implementing policies that raise incomes of workers and peasants as much as by exporting goods.

Although NAFTA is the model for FTAA, Mexico's experience is not inspiring. Timothy Wise from Tufts University's Global Development and Environment Institute recently reported that since Mexico began opening its markets, economic and job growth have been slow, job quality and wages have declined, poverty has increased, environmental quality has deteriorated, the rural sector is in crisis, and Mexico has a global balance of payments deficit despite its trade surplus with the United States. Corporations have used NAFTA's provision for investor lawsuits against governments to pursue—and typically win—millions of dollars in compensation from all three NAFTA governments for regulations designed to protect public health and the environment.

Free Marketeers Eye Brazil

Venezuela, which under Hugo Chavez has become the FTAA's fiercest critic, wants as a precondition the establishment of a development fund like the one the European Union established for integrating poorer member countries. Also, if the United States won't discuss its procedures to fight dumping or agriculture subsidies, then Brazil is not interested in discussing deregulation of services or investor protections. Meanwhile, Brazil is trying to consolidate Latin American trading relationships, while the United States is using a combination of threats and promises to establish bilateral trade relations with individual countries such as Chile and with smaller groups of countries like the Central American Free Trade Agreement, which may be completed this year.

The United States' veiled threats to negotiate FTAA without Brazil are hollow because that South American giant is the big corporate prize. "Going after bilaterals and the Central American Free Trade Agreement is all about getting Brazil, backing them into a corner and making them feel they have to give in," says Sarah Anderson, director of the global economy project at the Institute for Policy Studies.

While Bush has domestic political reasons to postpone negotiations, his corporate allies feel they're in a race against time. Popular resistance to the policies enshrined in FTAA is growing. "They figure if they don't lock it in now," says Lori Wallach, director of Public Citizens Global Trade Watch, "it won't be possible."

> *"Tying any modification in our unilateral embargo to the end of the Castro regime ... does us and the Cuban people a disservice."*

The United States Should Lift Its Cuban Embargo

Vicki Huddleston

In the following viewpoint, Vicki Huddleston maintains that since the U.S. embargo of Cuba has not put an end to the Communist regime, the United States should end the policy. If the United States continues to isolate Cuba, she argues, the people must depend on the Cuban government to change, an unlikely event since the government has been unwilling to change for fifty years. However, Huddleston adds, removing barriers and increasing communication with Cuba will reduce the people's dependence on the state and thus further the speed of change from within. Huddleston is a scholar of Latin America and Africa at the Brookings Institute.

Vicki Huddleston, "Cuba Embargo's Usefulness Has Run Its Course," *Miami Herald*, March 10, 2008. Republished with permission of *Miami Herald*, conveyed through Copyright Clearance Center, Inc.

As you read, consider the following questions:

1. What did the fact that Fidel Castro handpicked his successor confirm beyond any doubt, in Huddleston's opinion?

2. What does the author claim will begin once the United States deals with Cuba as one sovereign state to another?

3. What is more likely to happen if the United States waits too long to lift the embargo, according to the author?

If I were a betting woman, I would bet that if *The Miami Herald* were to ask Cuban Americans what U.S. foreign policy has been the least successful over the last half century, the overwhelming answer would be none other than: Cuba.

A Secure Legacy

No matter how much we may wish it to be otherwise, there is no denying the fact that Fidel Castro and the Cuba Revolution have survived and to some degree thrived, despite all our efforts to the contrary. If we had any doubt, it should have been removed when Fidel handed over power to his hand-picked loyal successor—his brother Raúl.

Ironically, Fidel has done that which we least expected—turn over power to a successor while he is still alive. But by doing so, he has ensured a peaceful transfer of power and his continuing influence within the regime's hierarchy. His legacy is secure—and he is still around to watch over it.

Raúl's job at 76 is to prepare for a transition to one of the loyal elite, such as Vice President Carlos Lage, Foreign Minister Felipe Roque, National Assembly President Ricardo Alarcón or even a lesser known such as the glamorous former head of the Cuban Interests Section in Washington D.C., Fernando Ramírez Estenoz.

If all goes well, Raúl will establish his legitimacy by carrying out modest reforms that put more food on the table, provide better housing and allow a bit more personal freedom.

Having waited so long for improved living conditions, Raúl may not have to do very much to boost his dour image and popularity. But if the revolution at any time appears to be in jeopardy, the older, harder, fighting men—including First Vice President José Ramón Machado Ventura, Gen. Julio Casas Regueiro, who replaced Raúl as minister of defense, and Minister of Interior Abelardo Colomé Ibarra—will bring the full force of the institutions they command to ensure their own survival and that of the Cuban state.

Removing the Barriers

There can no longer be any doubt that our isolation of Cuba did not and cannot bring about the end of the revolution. What will bring about the revolution's demise are old age, illness and death. More important, the revolution will evolve as it loses its founding fathers and becomes increasingly less isolated from its neighbors though the Internet, television, travelers and the flow of information.

But how fast and how far the revolution evolves depends upon U.S. policy. If we remove the barriers to communication, we will speed the forces of change. Just as was the case in Eastern Europe as a result of the Helsinki agreements, the Cuban people will be empowered by human contact, the free flow of information, and the support and encouragement of Americans and Cuban Americans from Florida to California.

If U.S. policy can deal with Cuba—not as a domestic political issue—but as one sovereign state to another, then we will resume official diplomatic relations with the exchange of ambassadors and begin—once again—to talk about matters that affect the well being and security of both our countries, namely migration, anti-narcotics, health and the environment. Starting a dialogue will allow us to press Cuba's leaders to respect the principles that we and the region hold dear: human rights, rule of law and freedom.

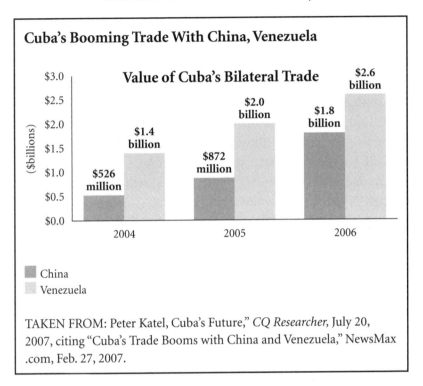

Cuba's Booming Trade With China, Venezuela

Value of Cuba's Bilateral Trade

China
Venezuela

TAKEN FROM: Peter Katel, Cuba's Future," *CQ Researcher*, July 20, 2007, citing "Cuba's Trade Booms with China and Venezuela," NewsMax .com, Feb. 27, 2007.

Removing the barriers to communications and to normal diplomatic relations are not concessions as some would claim. Rather, they are practical initiatives that will reduce the dependence of the Cuban people on the Cuban state by providing them with alternative sources of information and resources to improve their daily lives.

Building a Civil Society

More critically, a policy based on helping the Cuban people succeed would enable them to build civil society and begin a process of growing democracy from the bottom up.

But the [George W.] Bush administration is standing by its policy that Cuba must change first, tying any modification in our unilateral embargo to the end of the Castro regime. This does us and the Cuban people a disservice because it ties our policy to that of Raúl Castro's. By waiting for the Cuban regime to act, we make policy initiatives that would bring about change, dependent on the actions of the Cuban government.

The longer we wait the more likely that Cuba's new leaders will manage without us. In three to five years, Cuba, with help from foreign investors, will have exploited deep-sea oil and its sugar cane ethanol, adding billions to its annual revenues and making the island a net exporter of energy.

Worse, the longer we wait, the slower the process of change. If we want to play a role in Cuba's future, we must act now to encourage change in Cuba, by the Cuban people.

"To soften the current U.S. trade embargo against Cuba would send the wrong message."

Lifting the U.S. Embargo on Cuba Will Not Help Cubans

Jerry Haas

In the following viewpoint, Jerry Haas claims that lifting the U.S. trade embargo of Cuba will benefit the Communist regime not the Cuban people. Although the Cuban people are entitled to fair elections and freedom from abuse at the hands of their government, these changes must come from within to ensure true democratic reform, he contends. According to Haas, softening the U.S. stand against the Communist regime by lifting the trade embargo will send the wrong message. Haas is a columnist for the Georgia-based newspaper Athens Banner-Herald *and is involved in Christian ministry.*

As you read, consider the following questions:

1. Why does Haas believe that nothing will change in Cuba after Fidel Castro's recent retirement?

2. What one thing does the author claim stands out as one walks along the beaches of Cuba's north coast?

Jerry Haas, "Lifting U.S. Embargo Won't Help Cubans," *Athens Banner-Herald* (Athens, Georgia), March 2, 2008. www.onlineathens.com. Reproduced by permission.

3. What single thing can Cuba offer Russia in exchange for financial aid and oil, in the author's view?

It's now official. Fidel Castro has retired, and been replaced by his brother, Raul. As the former Cuban defense minister, Raul has the reputation of being a heavy-handed enforcer. After the 1959 revolution in which Castro forces deposed President Fulgencio Batista, Raul oversaw the execution of soldiers deemed to be Batista loyalists.

A few years ago, Raul was quoted as saying Cuba can be ruled in one way—"only the Communist Party." This shouldn't be a surprise, since Raul became a communist as a youth, well before his older brother Fidel embraced communism.

No Hope for Change

Many hope for change in Cuba with Fidel Castro retired, but change will not occur. The ruling circle is filled with the old guard communists. Raul now is their leader and will remain such until he decides to step down, or until some other internal upheaval results in a regime change. . . .

I went to Cuba. It is a country with beautiful flora and fauna, and a wonderful climate. However, these stand in stark contrast to the crumbling buildings, the poverty-stricken existence of the people, and a spirit of fear that permeates the culture. While lip service is given to freedom of religion, there is no freedom to assemble to worship except in a government-registered church.

Many food warehouses, located in local communities for the communistic distribution of food, stand empty. The basic staples of rice and beans fill other warehouses, awaiting distribution to the Communist Party faithful via the mandatory rationing system.

One thing that stands out as you walk along the pristine beaches of Cuba's north coast is the concrete bunkers. If they are there to stop a "yanqui" invasion, they will never be

---

Protecting National Security

What message would the United States be sending to oil-rich, tyrannical regimes around the world about the consequences of expropriation if we were now to lift the embargo that was imposed after Fidel Castro expropriated the assets of Esso, Shell and Texaco?

For many years the U.S. embargo has served to protect America's national security interests; today it is also serving to prevent Cuba's regime from drilling near U.S. shores.

Mauricio Claver-Carone, "How the Cuban Embargo Protects the Environment," International Herald Tribune, *July 25, 2008.*

---

manned during a single day of conflict. The coastal gun emplacements I saw are just as ridiculous. All of these defenses are just for show. There will be no U.S. invasion from the sea, and these meager defenses would never withstand the onslaught of modern warfare. Perhaps they are to be a comfort to the people, showing that the Cuban military stands ready to repel any foreign army. But the Cuban people, due to years of firsthand experience, know the military is used more for keeping people in Cuba than keeping foreign armies out.

Cuba's Trade Prospects

Venezuelan President Hugo Chavez is a great friend to Fidel Castro, but has not been as cozy with Raul. However, it wasn't long after Raul's election that he spoke with Chavez and was chatting live on the Venezuelan's television program. After all, Venezuela sells crude oil to Cuba at very favorable prices, in exchange for medical doctors from the island nation. Raul knows Cuba can't afford oil from other sources and will not risk jeopardizing the relationship.

Russia might once again become a strong Cuban ally and financier, now that Russian oil revenues are strengthening that country's economy. They certainly have oil, but Cuba has nothing of value to trade with Russia except its geographic location near the United States. With the recent plans by the U.S. to place part of our anti-ballistic missile system in the Czech Republic and Poland, right at the doorstep of Russia, what will prevent Russia from trying to deploy their own anti-ballistic missile system in Cuba? This would give the new Cuban leader negotiation leverage in his quest for more oil and financial aid.

Freedom from Within

The Cuban people have the same inalienable rights endowed by their creator as we in America. They deserve to have free and fair elections of a democratic government. Political prisoners must be set free and human rights abuses at the hands of government agents must cease. But these changes have to come from within Cuba, just as they came from within our original 13 colonies.

To soften the current U.S. trade embargo against Cuba would send the wrong message. For some reason, those supporting such action think the people of Cuba would benefit. Don't forget, Cuba is a communist nation, so it won't be the people of Cuba who benefit from a relaxation of the embargo. Any economic advantage will be sucked up by the communist regime and result in strengthening the stranglehold of communism on the general population. The communists will become more powerful, more abusive and more entrenched.

Whomever we elect as U.S. president in November [2008] might not be able to prod the changes within Cuba that will give them their freedom, but certainly could betray the Cuban people by relaxing the embargo before true democratic changes are in place.

> *"Instead of militarizing relations and building fortresses, the United States should address the reasons why majorities thoughout [Latin America] are turning against U.S.-led models."*

The United States Should Reduce Its Military Presence in Latin America

John Lindsay-Poland

In the following viewpoint, John Lindsay-Poland argues that instead of militarizing its relationship with Latin America, the United States should address the problems in the region that are promoting anti-American sentiment. Lindsay-Poland also claims that U.S. military support in Colombia contributes to the displacement of local populations and that human rights violations are on the rise. Lindsay-Poland is author of Emperors in the Jungle: The Hidden History of the U.S. in Panama.

As you read, consider the following questions:

1. How does the Pentagon use Honduras and El Salvador as "vassal states," according to Lindsay-Poland?

John Lindsay-Poland, "Yankees Head Home," *FPIF Policy Report*, March 6, 2008. Copyright © 2008 IRC and IPS. www.fpic.org. All rights reserved. Reproduced by permission.

2. How has the United States adapted to resistance to its military enclave system in Panama and Puerto Rico, in the author's opinion?

3. In the author's view, how has Washington responded to the tide of resistance to U.S. military presence in Argentina and Equador?

While visiting Italy [in] October [2007] Ecuadorean President Rafael Correa made a modest proposal: if the United States allows his country to set up a military base in Miami, his government would renew the lease for a U.S. base in the coast city of Manta. Otherwise, U.S. troops and operations will have to leave when the base lease ends next year.

Less than a month later, Correa passed through Miami on his way to China, and U.S. Customs police treated the president as an ordinary foreigner. It wasn't the first time Correa and his vice-president had been denied diplomatic treatment. Ecuador's foreign minister called the incident a "humiliation of a head of state, from arrogance by a country that believes itself above all others."

Declining U.S. Influence

Latin Americans are increasingly saying "No" to the U.S. military bases that are spread through the region. The Pentagon uses vassal states in Central America—Honduras and El Salvador—as bases for drug-war surveillance, police training, helicopter sorties, and military-run charity programs. And Colombia, a key ally in the region, receives more military equipment and training than the rest of the hemisphere combined.

But U.S. influence in the region is declining, and the U.S. military presence is perceived as protecting a failed economic model. Instead of militarizing relations and building fortresses, the United States should address the reasons why majorities throughout the region are turning against U.S-led models.

The widespread U.S. military presence in Latin America and the Caribbean has a long history. Bases resulted from and facilitated the hundreds of U.S. interventions to protect corporate property, coups, occupations, threats by gunboats, and other uses of force since the mid-1800s. Panama was carved out of Colombia in order to build the canal, with a series of bases and forts. In addition to protecting the canal, U.S. bases there served for training Latin American armies, preparing U.S. troops for jungle warfare in World War II and the Vietnam War, testing military equipment, including chemical weapons and preventing leftist forces from either winning or consolidating power in Central America.

The Dynamics in Panama and Puerto Rico

Advantages thus obtained by Panama, including access to U.S. markets through the Canal Zone, always conflicted with a desire for independence and with resentment of U.S. arrogance, racism, and interference. A similar dynamic occurred in Puerto Rico, where the Navy moved in after the Spanish-American War in 1898 and remained in the colony for more than a century.

The 1978 ratification of the Panama Canal Treaties, which required the United States to close its bases in Panama by the end of 1999, represented a watershed in U.S. policy, but Washington never renounced military hegemony in the hemisphere.

The enclave system of military basing in Panama and Puerto Rico—with thousands of troops, multiple military capacities, and internal societies alienated from the "host country"—has largely dissolved, with the possible and ironic exception of Guantánamo, as a result of popular resistance. But the United States has adapted by establishing more and smaller bases and "security locations," by relying on proxy troops trained and supplied by the United States, and by using air and naval forces for intelligence.

The U.S. Presence in Colombia, Honduras, and Guantánamo

The largest bastion of U.S. military presence is in Colombia, where 800 soldiers and 600 military contractors are supporting a counterinsurgency that targets civilians and destroying health and environment through aerial fumigation as part of the failed so-called "Drug War."

Then the United States operates a base in Soto Cano, Honduras, set up in 1984. It's a legacy of [the Ronald] Reagan administration's efforts to prevent a leftist revolution in El Salvador while fighting the Sandinista government in Nicaragua by subsidizing, in violation of a congressionally imposed ban, the armed *contra* insurgents. The Soto Cano base provides support for training and helicopter sorties. And there's an air base and police training academy in El Salvador. And drug traffic surveillance facilities in Curazao and Aruba.

The infamous detention camp in Guantánamo, Cuba is in fact part of a longstanding U.S. naval base there, which enjoys a lease with no termination date. With an uninterrupted U.S. presence since 1903, Guantánamo has served as a rest and relaxation site for sailors and Marines, refueling site for Coast Guard ships and temporary camp for Haitian refugees. The military detention camp established for detainees of suspected Al Qaeda members, in violation of Geneva Convention norms, where documented torture and abuse are rife, currently overshadows the naval base, which is controversial in its own right. The base is a hangover from the earlier heyday [of] U.S. imperialism a century ago, and Cuba has refused to deposit U.S. Treasury checks for the base's below-market rent.

Widespread Withdrawal

Revulsion toward U.S. unilateralism and the torture methods used and taught by U.S. officials is leading to withdrawal from some U.S.-run military programs, such as the U.S. School of the Americas (relocated from Panama in 1984; now called the Western Hemisphere Institute for Security Cooperation).

Bases set up in Puerto Rico and Ecuador, partly as a result of the closure of bases in Panama, are already closed or soon will be. The grassroots movement of civil disobedience, culture, and political action to stop the naval bombing in Vieques, Puerto Rico unified a colonized society otherwise fractured by attitudes towards relations with the United States. Ecuador bowed out of hosting a multinational naval exercise last year [in 2007], and several Latin American nations have refused to sign agreements that would exempt U.S. soldiers from prosecution in the International Criminal Court.

Argentina even led a multinational military exercise in October 2006 "to recover an airport that has fallen under the control of an extra-continental power, being used to fly in and deploy troops into the area." The United States is the only such power with the capacity and political wherewithal to fly in troops in such an operation. Paraguayan soldiers participated in the exercise, dubbed "Operación Hermandad" (Operation Brotherhood).

Washington's Response

Washington's response to this rising tide of resistance increasingly has been to rely on Colombia, where President Alvaro Uribe is George W. Bush's Latin political twin. Colombia harbors 1,400 U.S. soldiers and military contractors, as well as five radar sites, all operated by the ITT Corporation, and a "Forward Operating Site" in Apiay. Apiay is one of a handful of sites in Colombia where the U.S. Army 7th Special Forces Group trains thousands of Colombian soldiers every year. Washington has appropriated $5.5 billion in mostly military funds since 2000 as part of "Plan Colombia," a bi-partisan initiative purportedly aimed at "going to the source" of cocaine production by fumigating coca fields. In reality it has been a

Deepening Divisions

Although the FARC [the Revolutionary Armed Forces of Colombia] is a major nemesis of the Colombian government, the militarization of the conflict since the rise to power of Uribe has dimmed prospects of peaceful resolution. Continuous scandals involving evidence of the government's close ties to paramilitary groups have deepened divisions. The arming of both sides—in large part as a result of U.S. military aid under Plan Colombia—has heightened the violence.

Laura Carlsen,
"The Andean Crisis and the Geopolitics of Trade,"
Americas Policy Program Commentary
(Washington, DC: Center for International Policy),
March 25, 2008. www.americas.inc-online.org.

project that helps Colombia's military fight insurgents. Drug trafficking has continued apace since the plan's inception.

Pundits repeatedly frame the prospect of reducing the U.S. military's presence in Colombia or rejecting the corporate-sponsored free trade agreement with the country as "abandoning a friend." "The danger for the United States is that if it abandons these Latin advocates of open markets, the beneficiaries will be radical supporters of Venezuela's Chávez," wrote David Ignatius in his *Washington Post* column. "Failing to ratify the [trade] agreement would be tantamount to abandoning a neighbor in its time of greatest need. . . . We desire nothing more than to give Colombia a pledge of economic trust and friendship," opined the *Los Angeles Times* in an editorial.

What Friends Are These?

But just what friends are these? Colombia's armed forces have allied with paramilitary death squads that have forced millions of Colombians to flee in terror from lands that are then occupied by others, and the army itself is the most abusive in the hemisphere. More than 75 of Uribe's circle of political colleagues and appointed officials are under investigation for working with paramilitary forces, while the Uribe government has worked out an amnesty for demobilized paramilitaries that has reinforced impunity.

Colombia remains the most dangerous country in the world for trade unionists, with more of them killed in 2006 than the rest of the world combined. Uribe consistently responds to criticism by political opponents and human rights workers by claiming it comes from the guerrillas. This is the model that the White House has been touting on Congressional junkets to Medellin in its drive to win approval of the Colombia trade agreement.

Colombia's militarization makes its neighbors nervous. The U.S. military base in Manta, Ecuador, set up with up to 500 US soldiers to run counter-drug flights when Panama threw out military bases in 1999, has become a controversial presence that a majority of Ecuadoreans want closed. The U.S. commander in Manta has also stated that the base is "very important" for Plan Colombia. U.S. officials defend the Manta base, asserting that drug traffic in Ecuador and the eastern Pacific has grown in recent years. But if drug traffic has grown since the base began operations in Manta in 2000, it suggests—at the very least—that it's ineffective.

Cutting Off Manta

President Rafael Correa, who was inaugurated [in 2007], pledged that his government would not maintain the lease for the Manta base, which expires in 2009, unless the United States allows Ecuador to have a military base in Florida. In a public letter to Correa, more than 40 peace, religious and solidarity organizations publicly declared their support in October [2007] for Ecuador's decision to close the US military base in Manta. "Every dollar spent on military approaches to drugs represents a theft from programs for at-risk youth and treatment of addiction in the United States, for investment in reducing U.S. carbon emissions, and for payment of other debts our country owes to the world," the groups said.

Keeping the air base in Manta is still on the table, say spokesmen at the Southern Command [U.S. military forces in South and Central America] and U.S. Embassy in Quito [Ecuador]. One arrangement that SouthCom is exploring would allow U.S. military or surveillance aircraft to land in Ecuador, but not at a fixed U.S. base.

The conflict that erupted between Colombia and Ecuador after Colombian forces bombed a FARC guerrilla camp in Ecuadorean territory on March 1 [2008] was born of rising bilateral tensions. Previous Colombian military operations along the border spurred diplomatic protest notes [in 2007]. When Ecuador [in May 2007] withdrew from annual naval exercises led by the United States that were scheduled to be held off its coastline, the U.S. Southern Command said that the exercises would be held instead in Malaga Bay on Colombia's Pacific coast. The Manta base houses AWACS aircraft with a capability for detecting satellite phone calls. The location of the FARC guerrilla camp was reportedly determined by a satellite call regarding humanitarian exchange of prisoners made by guerrilla leader Raul Reyes to Senator Piedad Cordoba, leading Ecuadorean groups to call for an investigation into the role that U.S. and Colombian soldiers based in Manta played in the operation.

The War on Drugs

The announced departure from Manta requires the Southern Command to go looking elsewhere in the region for a spot to base its air operations. The two candidates leaked to the media are Peru and Colombia. The United States already conducts extensive military activities in both countries. Peru hosts a key radar station used in the "War on Drugs," and the United States has expanded the tempo of military maneuvers in the country. Moving the operations to Colombia would consolidate the country's position as the Latin American country most militarized by the United States.

The failed militarized approach to traffic in illegal drugs hasn't affected the availability or price of these drugs in U.S. communities, nor addressed the poverty and lack of infrastructure that leads some Latin American farmers to enter the illegal economy. A study by the Rand Corporation showed that spending on treatment of drug users is more than ten times as effective for reducing illegal drug use as interdiction of the sort conducted from the Manta base.

What's Good for DynCorp

The premise of the policy, that revving up the Colombian military to fight the guerrillas who protect coca plantations will affect the street price of cocaine, has been thoroughly discredited. So we might ask: Who, besides the corrupt Colombian military, has benefited from the $5.5 billion appropriated for Plan Colombia since 2000? The No. 1 beneficiaries in dollars are the U.S. companies that produce Blackhawk gunships and run the program of chemical warfare in Colombia's coca fields. These include the companies providing the U.S. government with "services" to aid the Drug War.

DynCorp International has signed contracts with the State Department for about $150 million annually since 2000 for its operations in Colombia. It also handles most of the operations at the Manta base. The company's corporate offices, like those of many of the growing band of mercenary outfits, are located in suburban Virginia, outside Washington. (The company's headquarters are in Falls Church, which is adjacent to the Congressional district of Representative Frank Wolf, the ranking Republican on the House of Representatives Foreign Operations subcommittee that marks up the hundreds of millions of dollars in funds that Congress approves for DynCorp.) The company in turn has consistently given thousands of dollars to Wolf's campaign. Such a blatant conflict of interest is another demonstration of Plan Colombia's corrupt underlying dynamics, which should be cause for a fundamental re-casting of the policy.

If the 2008 elections yield a Democratic victory, renewing the party's majority in Congress and winning the presidency, the next administration will get a chance to not only re-examine the premises of failed economic, military and narcotics policies in Latin America, but to re-shape those policies to engage the new majorities emerging throughout the region. Democrats, to be true to democratic values, should undertake such a fundamental shift in policy. But don't hold your breath. Democrats and Republicans are likely to only react reflexively, unless people in the United States actively press them to do so.

> "The best way for Washington to guard against ... [Chinese influence] is not to inflate the Chinese threat but to re-engage with Latin America, rebuilding a comprehensive relationship with this region."

The United States Should Counteract China's Influence in Latin America

Joshua Kurlantzick

In the following viewpoint, Joshua Kurlantzick maintains that China's influence in Latin America is growing, and that the country hopes to ensure access to the region's resources while also thinning Taiwan's ties. Moreover, Kurlantzick claims, China hopes to appear a more cooperative partner than the United States. The best way for the United States to check China's growing influence is to focus less on counterterrorism and more on the problems facing a broader base of the Latin American population, he asserts. Kurlantzick is a foreign policy scholar and the author of Charm Offensive: How China's Soft Power Is Transforming the World.

Joshua Kurlantzick, "China's Latin Leap Forward," *World Policy Journal*, vol. 23, Fall 2006, pp. 33–41. Copyright © 2006 World Policy Institute. Reproduced by permission of The MIT Press, Cambridge, MA.

As you read, consider the following questions:

1. According to Kurlantzick, why did Hu Jintao's Latin American visit surprise U.S. policymakers?

2. In the author's view, how has the perception of China changed in Latin America in the last fifteen years?

3. How could China end up looking little different from the old colonial powers to Latin Americans, in the author's opinion?

In fall 2004, the president of China, Hu Jintao, embarked upon a trip to Latin America that sometimes seemed more a coronation than a diplomatic offensive. In Brazil, Chile, Cuba, and Argentina, Hu was received with the highest honors of a state guest, while local legislators battled to hold receptions for him and for the delegation of Chinese businesses searching for new investments in the region. Latin businesspeople hosted Hu at barbeques and welcomed him into their factories. Latin leaders recognized China as a market economy, one of Beijing's major goals, and lavished praise on Hu, with the Brazilian president, Luiz Inacio Lula da Silva, announcing, "We want a partnership that integrates our economies and serves as a paradigm for South-South cooperation."

Hu also delivered concrete signs of China's growing relationship with Latin America. The Chinese leader signed $30 billion worth of new investment deals, upgraded bilateral trade ties with Brazil and announced an "all-weather strategic partnership" with the Latin giant, and signed some 400 agreements with Latin American nations on a range of topics. Shortly after Hu's trip, Chinese vice president Zeng Qinghong led his own entourage of Chinese officials and business leaders to Latin America, where they signed a new deal on oil and gas exploration with Caracas and offered Venezuela $700 million in credits.

Hu's grand tour of Latin America surprised many U.S. policymakers and opinion leaders, who have long considered the region the United States' natural sphere of influence, and who have not contended with another external competitor in the region in decades. An article published in *Foreign Affairs* wondered if Washington was "losing Latin America." A Senate aide told the *New York Times*, "They're taking advantage of it. They're taking advantage of the fact that we don't care as much as we should about Latin America." Congress convened hearings to examine China's presence in the Western Hemisphere, and the White House instituted a dialogue with China to explore the two powers' aims in the region.

Behind China's Offensive

In truth, neither the accolades for Hu nor the fears of China's presence in the Western Hemisphere accurately capture the current state of Beijing's dynamic new engagement with Latin America. China clearly has a strategy designed to increase its influence in developing regions—Southeast Asia, Central Asia, Africa, and Latin America—because Beijing believes it can wield greater influence there than in developed nations in Northeast Asia, Europe, and the United States.

China has enjoyed considerable success in achieving its initial goals in Latin America, which include revamping Beijing's global image, isolating Taiwan, and securing access to commodities, among other targets. At this point, China has made few difficult demands on countries in Latin America, so, for now, nations in the region get a free ride from China's involvement, benefiting from aid, investment, and diplomacy without having to make significant sacrifices to win Beijing's favor. Yet, as China expands its presence in Latin America, many of its policies could risk a backlash, lessening its ability to threaten U.S. interests in the region. . . .

China's Goals and Strategies

Since 2001, China's goals, strategies, and tools of influence in Latin America have come into clearer focus. As in its relations with developing regions like Southeast Asia, China has several obvious goals. China wants to ensure its access to the region's oil, gas, copper, iron, and other important resources. Unlike most Western energy companies, which operate independently from the state and rely on global markets to set prices, many Chinese firms retain close ties to the government, which distrusts global energy markets.

Chinese leaders fear that, in a conflict with the United States, Washington might be able to cut off international supply lanes or pressure American allies not to supply China. Consequently, Chinese firms search for equity stakes in oil overseas and try to "secure the entire supply chain in critical industries," according to one observer. In other words, China wants to control the entire process, from oil field to tanker. And Latin America is the current center of China's global strategy.

China also clearly seeks to diminish Taiwan's formal and informal ties to Latin America, a region where Taiwan still retains formal links with Panama, Paraguay, and Guatemala, among others. In addition, China wants nations that already recognize Beijing to not only adhere to the One China policy but also to prevent Taiwanese officials from participating in nongovernmental regional forums like the Organization of American States. China also may wish to prevent governments from entering into bilateral free trade deals with the island.

Beijing also intends to promote itself as a benign, cooperative presence—as a different, more accommodating external power than the United States. If China is perceived as a benign actor, as a nation that does not threaten the region economically or militarily, it will be easier for Beijing to expand trade, boost its diplomatic offensive, and even broaden military-military cooperation such as selling arms, securing strategic shipping lanes, and developing joint training programs with nations like Venezuela. Ultimately, Beijing might even be able to use its engagement with the region to diminish U.S. influence in the Western Hemisphere, or at least pressure Washington to commit more resources to the hemisphere—resources that might otherwise be deployed in Beijing's backyard, Southeast and Northeast Asia. . . .

Measuring China's Progress

For now, China's strategies and tools of influence appear to be working. Beijing has successfully decreased Taiwan's formal and informal relationships in Latin America. In addition to convincing Dominica and Grenada to switch recognition, China has opened commercial relations with Guatemala, often the first step towards switching recognition. China also has opened a commercial office in Haiti, another Taiwanese ally, and kept Taiwan from obtaining observer status at the Organization of American States; Haiti, Panama, and the Dominican Republic no longer support Taiwan's presence in the United Nations. Within a decade, Taiwan may well have no formal allies in Latin America.

Beijing also has boosted trade ties. Trade volumes between China and the hemisphere have grown from only $200 million in 1975 to roughly $50 billion in 2005, though the United States accounts for more than 40 percent of Latin American exports. The tide is turning, however: Argentina's exports to China rose by more than 40 percent between 1998 and 2004; Venezuela's exports to China over that same period grew by more than 19 percent; and Colombia's exports grew by nearly 10 percent. China still lags far behind U.S. trade with the region, however—the United States normally accounts for half of total Latin American trade, while China is less than 5 percent. The United States' annual investment in Latin America ordinarily tops $30 billion; China's total investment is still less than $5 billion. . . .

Perhaps most important, Beijing has convinced much of Latin America that it can be a benign and constructive actor, a drastic change from regional perceptions of China only 15 years ago, when it was either not on radar screens or was

The Stakes Are High in Colombia

A race is on for influence and, ultimately, for power in the Western Hemisphere. Strangers from the Eastern Hemisphere, from China to Russia, from Europe to Iran, are interested in trade and secure supplies of resources, minerals, and energy. These less constrained outsiders with little oversight arrive daily in places like Bogota and Panama City with new offers for trade and investment. While we elect to sit on the sidelines, others move to cut deals and cut us out.

James M. Roberts and Ray Walser,
"Losing Latin America? A Protectionist Congress
Is Destroying U.S. Credibility," Web Memo #1890,
Heritage Foundation, April 15, 2008. www.heritage.org.

viewed by many as a rising threat. Limited polling suggests that most of the hemisphere enjoys a generally positive view of China. Even in Mexico, whose export sectors compete directly with China and whose press has highlighted the negative impact of China's economic growth on Mexican textiles and other industries, a comprehensive opinion survey taken in 2004 shows that Mexicans worry about Chinese economic competition but that "the development of China as a world power rank[s] at the bottom of the list of threats that Mexicans consider critical."

This sentiment potentially boosts Beijing's influence. In democratic nations, leaders can move closer to China, since public sentiment supports better relations, including, potentially, closer military ties. In less democratic nations, like Venezuela, where a small circle of elites make decisions, China's appeal serves the same function, allowing them to build consensus on warmer relations with Beijing.

How Much of a Threat?

Despite China's successful engagement with Latin America, its growing presence in the region does not necessarily yet threaten U.S. interests. Thus far, there are few signs that Beijing seeks to directly challenge Washington's substantial military relationship with Latin America. On his trip to Latin America in 2004, Hu Jintao did not visit Colombia, perhaps because he did not want to be seen meddling with the closest U.S. ally in South America.

Some of China's relations in the region could benefit Washington. China's growing economic relationship with Latin America may prompt Beijing to take a stronger interest in regional security and thus share important regional burdens with the United States. Indeed, as China becomes more influential, it could help mediate conflicts, as it has done with North Korea in Northeast Asia. It also may play a larger role in peacekeeping operations, as China has already begun to do in Haiti. In addition, as China absorbs more of Latin America's resources, it will provide funds for Latin governments to pay off their external debts, reducing the possibility of further financial instability in the region, potentially diminishing the flow of Latin America's economic migrants.

Despite its initial gains, though, China could flounder, as Latin Americans learn more about its strategies. Less than two years after China and Brazil's courtship, strains have developed in Beijing's relationship with the largest nation in South America as a flood of Chinese imports has not been matched by Chinese consumption of Brazilian goods. Other Latin American nations echo the same complaint. Argentina has imposed new non-tariff barriers on categories of Chinese imports. Moreover, many opinion leaders perceive Beijing as an unfair competitor, due to Chinese labor practices, dumping, undervaluing its currency, and state support for certain industries. . . .

Eventually, Beijing could end up looking little different to Latin Americans than the old colonial powers, who mined and dug up the region, doing nothing to improve the capacity of locals, if Chinese investment focuses on extractive industries and adds little to the skills of the local workforce, the region could become trapped in a pattern of mercantilism with China, in which it sells natural resources to buy higher-value manufactured goods, without developing a cadre of local-country managers for Chinese firms.

Latin American leaders and publics also recognize that China's supposed dedication to developing nations is not always trustworthy, and that China's economic model may prove no more effective than the neo-liberal model. China's own socioeconomic inequalities have exposed some of the failings of Sino-style development. Some scholars even express concerns about the "Latin Americanization" of China—i.e. that China is becoming as economically unequal as Latin America.

China's push could eventually constitute a threat to U.S. political, security, and economic interests. China's focus on energy could complicate U.S. access to resources. Global reserves of cheaply obtainable oil are decreasing rapidly, and Latin American imports—particularly from Venezuela—are among the nearest and cheapest for the United States. Since reserves in most of Latin America are projected to begin declining by the end of this decade, these imports will become even more crucial to U.S. energy needs. Venezuela has not only threatened to cut off all U.S. shipments but also has said that it plans to boost exports to China from the current 140,000 barrels of crude oil per day to 500,000 barrels.

Even as Venezuela increases shipments to China, U.S. demand for oil is unlikely to decrease—forecasts suggest imports could rise by as much as 60 percent in the next 20 years. Growing U.S. demand, combined with a shift in Venezuelan exports, could force Washington to become vastly more dependent on Middle Eastern oil. This has obvious security consequences. . . .

Counteracting Chinese Influence

Worse, if Beijing's influence undermines democratization in Latin America, it could bolster authoritarian leaders in the region. Finding another major source of economic assistance and diplomatic support might allow actors like Chavez more freedom to undermine U.S. counternarcotics and counterterrorism initiatives in, for example, Colombia.

The best way for Washington to guard against these possibilities, however, is not to inflate the Chinese threat but to re-engage with Latin America, rebuilding a comprehensive relationship with this region—not only with a few key allies like Colombia. China's success in the Western Hemisphere derives in good part from failed U.S. policies, such as an overemphasis on counterterrorism and overreliance on a small number of conservative leaders to make policy in the region.

Such a renewed relationship could begin by addressing what Latin America scholar Julia Sweig calls the "80/20 problem," in which Washington relies on elites—20 percent of the population—to understand entire countries. Interacting with the "other" 80 percent of populations, including more contacts with non-governmental organizations, political activists, advocates for the poor, and religious leaders, would foster deeper ties.

Washington also could re-emphasize core U.S. strengths. When Latin Americans perceive the United States as helping them achieve a free, rights-oriented system, America's appeal in the region surges. As Sweig [director for Latin America Studies, Council on Foreign Relations] writes, during the 1990s Washington often "set forth a positive agenda" in Latin America by backing civil societies recovering from years of war and promoting democracy. "Latin America welcomed the new approach . . . the message from the North was largely positive, inclusive, and respectful," Sweig notes. If Washington returned to that approach, China's leap forward would surely slow down.

Periodical Bibliography

The following articles have been selected to supplement the diverse views presented in this chapter.

Laura Carlsen — "The Andean Crisis and the Geopolitics of Trade," American Policy Program, Center for International Policy, March 25, 2008.

Council on Foreign Relations — "U.S.-Latin America Relations: A New Direction for a New Reality," Independent Task Force Report No. 60, 2008.

Daniel P. Erickson — "Requiem for the Monroe Doctrine," *Current History*, February 2008.

Alan M. Field — "Grand Illusion? (Trade Agreements Between United States, Latin America, South America)," *Journal of Commerce*, April 7, 2008.

Carlos M. Gutierrez — "Cuba at the Crossroads," *Heritage Lectures*, October 24, 2007.

Kiraz Janicke — "War vs. Peace: Colombia, Venezuela and the FARC Hostage Saga," *venezuelanalysis.com*, February 8, 2008. www.venezuelanalysis.com/analysis/3134.

Peter Katel — "Cuba's Future," *CQ Researcher*, July 20, 2007.

Shannon K. O'Neil — "A New Direction in Latin America," *Washington Post*, May 30, 2008.

Michelle Quiles — "Cuba Under Raúl Castro: 25 Reasons to Be Hopeful," Council on Hemispheric Affairs, June 23, 2008. www.coha.org.

James M. Roberts and Ray Walser — "Losing Latin America? A Protectionist Congress Is Destroying U.S. Credibility," *WebMemo* [Heritage Foundation], April 15, 2008.

Mark Weisbrot — "Gap Between Latin America and Washington Still Growing," *AlterNet*, June 13, 2008.

CHAPTER 4

What Is the Status of Human Rights in Latin America?

Chapter Preface

One of several controversies concerning human rights in Latin America is the dispute over the region's multiracial ideal. According to MIT professor Melissa Nobles, elites in many Latin American nations claim to celebrate the mixing of races and to extend equal rights and opportunities to all citizens, regardless of race. "It has long been widely assumed that Latin American societies are nondiscriminatory and that their deep economic and social disparities have no racial or ethnic component," Nobles maintains. She observes, however, that the region's multiracial ideal has come into question. Indeed, many analysts claim that one of the serious human rights problems in Latin America is deeply seated racial inequality and discrimination.

According to a 2006 World Bank study, an estimated 150 million African descendants live in Latin America, making them the largest ethnic group in the region. While these citizens comprise about 30 percent of the population, they make up more than half of the poor. In fact, race is one of the most persistent predictors of poverty in the region. The Latin American country with the largest African descendant population is Brazil, whose official Human Development Index (HDI) ranking is 69, meaning that there are 68 nations worldwide that have a higher HDI. The HDI measures factors such as life expectancy, literacy, educational attainment, and gross domestic product. If, however, Brazil's HDI ranking were based on its Afro-Brazilian population alone, Brazil would rank 101. If its HDI were based on its white population alone, Brazil would rank 46. Scholars in organizations devoted to improving human development contend that racism in the region squanders its most valuable resource—its people. According to Judith Morrison, regional director for South America and the Caribbean at the Inter-American Foundation, "Brazil and other Latin America economies could expand by over one third, if people of colour were fully included in the workforce of their nations."

Although governments and international organizations have focused attention on programs to address the concerns of the indigenous population, the racial problem remains largely ignored, "even though there is growing evidence that race is a key factor in the distribution of income, wealth, and public services," Morrison maintains. One explanation for the region's failure to address racial inequities is what some term the myth of multiracialism. Historical figures, such as Mexican educator and philosopher José Vasconcelos, celebrated racial mixture, proclaiming Latin Americans a *raza cosmica* (cosmic race). This ideal of racial democracy has flourished in Latin America even when political democracy has not. Indeed, Nobles asserts, "The rhetoric of multiracialism has routinely been deployed by oligarchic and authoritarian regimes." As democratic institutions grew during the 1980s and 1990s in Latin America, however, the reality of racial inequality remained. "As democracy becomes more real in the region, however slowly, the unreality of racial democracy becomes ever more obvious," Nobles contends. Unless addressed, some critics reason, the reality of racial inequality will continue to hurt the region. "The continuing lack of attention to pervasive socio-economic gaps must be addressed or Latin America as a whole will lag behind other regions of the world," Morrison concludes.

Whether Latin America will address racial inequities or continue to mask racial injustice with an unrealized multiracial ideal remains to be seen. The authors in the following chapter debate other questions concerning human rights in Latin America.

> *"Security forces [in Latin America] con-*
> *tinue to violate the rights of civilians at*
> *alarming rates, with impunity."*

Human Rights Violations Persist in Latin America

Eric L. Olson

In the following viewpoint, Eric L. Olson claims that despite eco-
nomic growth and improvements in governance, human rights
violations in Latin America persist. Although elected civilian
governments have replaced military regimes, security forces con-
tinue to violate civilian rights with impunity, he asserts. In fact,
Olson adds, the failure of civilian forces has led to a demand for
remilitarization in some Latin American nations. Olson is advo-
cacy director for the Americas at Amnesty International USA
and has lived in Venezuela, Honduras, and Mexico.

As you read, consider the following questions:

1. According to Olson, what has been the impact of the "mano dura" in El Salvador and Honduras?

2. How have the traditional political parties in most Latin American countries been replaced, in the author's view?

Eric L. Olson, "Divided States of the Americas: Human Rights and Democracy in Latin America: A Progress Report," *Sojourners Magazine*, vol. 35, March 2006, pp. 29–32. Copyright © 2006 *Sojourners*. Reproduced with permission from *Sojourners*. (800) 714-7474. www.sojo.net.

3. Whose rights have received renewed attention in Latin America, in the author's opinion?

A recent trip to the U.S.-Mexico border brought to mind the old saying that the more things change, the more they remain the same. I was traveling with a congressional delegation to look into the murders of nearly 400 young women in Ciudad Juarez and Chihuahua since 1993. The area was transformed by passage of the North American Free Trade Agreement (NAFTA), which proponents promised would be a "win-win" for Mexico and the United States—more jobs would bring increased wealth, which in turn would bring greater stability to the area and lessen migratory pressures.

Telling Half the Story

Economic activity and cross-border trade did increase dramatically along the border as state-of-the-art assembly plants ("maquilas") were built. But the slick NAFTA propaganda told only half the story. As we traveled from the modern offices of the city's "maquila" association to the communities where workers live, the crushing poverty was unmistakable. Unpaved streets were caked with the thick, gritty accumulated dust and grime of the surrounding desert. Old shipping crates and scraps were carefully assembled into houses and perched precariously on a denuded hillside. Some lucky residents had running water and one electrical line to illuminate their house; no one had heat to protect against the chill howling desert winds.

Just over the hill on a distant range, the bodies of young women were found, often showing signs of severe sexual torture. These murders are a vivid reminder that even in modern Mexico where trade and economic opportunities are growing, poor people, especially women, are vulnerable to violence and can expect very little from the authorities, who themselves are often implicated in the brutality.

Although there are similarities, the point is not to make Ciudad Juarez a microcosm of what is happening throughout the rest of Central and South America, but rather to illustrate that dramatic changes in the region over the past 20 years have not resolved many of the underlying factors that gave rise to social and political unrest and armed conflict of the recent past.

Lessons Not Learned

Two of the most important changes in Latin America since the 1980s have been the gradual transition from armed struggles and military dictatorships to elected civilian governments in nearly every country; and "economic modernization" with its free market- and free trade-oriented policies demanded by Washington. Despite these changes, security forces continue to violate the rights of civilians at alarming rates, with impunity. Polls suggest that a majority of Latin Americans have little faith in their democratic governments and institutions. And as the example of Ciudad Juarez suggests, poverty and economic disparity remain unchecked.

While the absence of military governments in Latin America is clearly a positive sign, the lessons learned from the era of military rule seem to be evaporating quickly. Disgraced militaries that left power in the 1980s are re-emerging as powerful actors in the region. Civilian authorities are once again calling upon their armed forces to involve themselves in internal security matters. Militaries are now involved in policing streets and combating organized crime in Mexico, Brazil, and Guatemala and confronting indigenous social movements throughout the Andean region.

The Remilitarization Trend

Popular demands for greater public safety, and the failings of civilian police forces—which are generally understood to be corrupt, abusive, and ineffective—often have resulted in citizen support for remilitarization. The trend is most visible in Central America, Mexico, and Colombia, where the popular appeal of dealing with serious social problems with the mano dura (iron fist) is undeniable. For instance, El Salvador and Honduras have increasingly used the mano dura to deal with the problem of youth gangs and public security. Draconian laws criminalize entire sectors of society for merely wearing a tattoo. Tough sentencing has led to even further overcrowding of grossly inadequate and inhumane jails.

"Not surprisingly, recent studies conducted in Central America suggest that the mano dura has done little to weaken the gang phenomenon, and has likely contributed to an increase in violence," said Geoff Thale of the Washington Office on Latin America (WOLA), an independent policy and advocacy group.

The United States has encouraged expanded roles for the military, initially for greater cooperation in its "War on Drugs." But the U.S. interest has now pushed beyond the expanded drug mission. "U.S. and Latin American militaries are spending considerable effort defining a list of current or 'emerging' threats such as gangs, drugs, organized crime, illegal migration, and natural disasters," according to Erasing the Lines, a December 2005 joint study by WOLA and other policy groups. The study continues, "while all are serious problems in the region, none are the kinds of threat that lend themselves to military solutions."

Questioning Democracy

While the role of the military expands, democracy itself has also come under increasing question. In a recent poll by a Chilean organization, Latinobarometro, citizens in 12 of the region's countries had a lower opinion of democracy in 2005 than they had in 1996; only 26 percent of respondents believed that there was equality before the law in their country;

one in five expressed any confidence in political parties; one in four trusted their legislature or the courts.

The experience with democracy has not been uniformly positive. In many countries, military dictators were replaced by traditional parties headed by political and economic elites that readily adopted pro-Washington trade and economic policies. As billions of dollars in foreign investment poured into the region, and billions more were made through the privatization of state-owned enterprises, corruption grew, and with it greater exclusion of Latin America's poor. The so-called modernization, or neo-liberal, reforms adopted throughout the region meant an influx of consumer goods from abroad, and declining government investment in education, public health, and agriculture. Poor and working-class Latin Americans saw the cost of basics increase while access to quality health and education services decreased.

This widespread social, economic, and political exclusion, which makes the region the most inequitable in the world, is one of the greatest unresolved challenges confronting the Americas. Dr. Enrique Iglesias, the former president of the Inter-American Development Bank [IDB], has said that, "as the region with the greatest level of inequality in the world, Latin America has the most to gain (from social inclusion)." The IDB's own studies found that those "countries with large indigenous or Afro-descendent populations would obtain immense social and economic gains by ending exclusion that permeates their health and education systems, as well as their labor markets."

While each country in the Americas has confronted the challenges of democracy and inequality in its own way, there are some emerging regional trends. In most countries, traditional parties have been swept aside and replaced by strong charismatic leaders. Only a handful of the region's current leaders were elected with the help of historic traditional parties. Brazil's Luis Ignacio Lula da Silva and Mexico's Vicente

A Continuing Problem

Even with the election of civilian governments and the greater application of the rule of law in most of the region, violations of basic human rights continue. In some countries, the press has been harassed and persecuted for uncovering human rights abuses, corruption, or other government scandals. There are many cases of horrific prison conditions and police brutality. Violence against women, indigenous peoples, and the poor remains far too common.

Christopher L. Brown and Alyssa Smith,
"Lesson 5: Poverty, Human Rights, and Social Change,"
Latin America in Transition,
Southern Center for International Studies, 2008.
www.southerncenter.org.

Fox may be the biggest exceptions, but both presidents are enormously charismatic figures, with Lula coming to personify Brazil's working class and Fox working hard to distance himself from his own party during his historic election in 2000.

A Trend Toward Authoritarianism

A closely related trend is toward authoritarianism. Once again, polls conducted by Latinobarometro suggest that the "military" is tied with the "presidency" as the most trusted institution of government, receiving a 41 percent approval rating in 2005. It's not surprising, then, that charismatic leaders in Colombia, Venezuela, Peru, and Mexico have sought alliances with the military to address pressing social and political problems.

Authoritarianism is also evident in efforts to further centralize power in the presidency by weakening other branches of government. In Venezuela, the Chavez government replaced dozens of justices with temporary appointees that could potentially be removed quickly if they ruled against the interests of the government. In Ecuador, then President [Lucio] Gutierrez fired the Supreme Court and replaced it with political allies. The subsequent public outcry forced him to reinstate the original court, but by then it was too late, and his government fell shortly thereafter.

There are also exceptions. The governments of Argentina, Chile, and Peru are trying mightily to bring past dictators to justice. The Chilean Supreme Court recently stripped Gen. Augusto Pinochet of immunity for human rights violations, and the 90-year-old former dictator is expected to stand trial if his health doesn't fail first [Pinochet died in December 2006, before he could be tried in court]. Likewise, the Peruvian government is seeking the extradition from Chile of its authoritarian former leader Alberto Fujimori to stand trial for 12 counts of human rights abuses and other crimes.

A third trend in the region is a movement toward "progressive populism," particularly in the Southern Cone of South America (Brazil, Uruguay, Argentina, Chile) and parts of the Andes (Venezuela and Bolivia, and possibly Ecuador and Peru in the near future). It's difficult to generalize about this trend because each country has a unique experience and philosophy of government. But from the free-market oriented socialist president of Chile, Ricardo Lagos (and his successor, Michelle Bachelet, who will take office in March [2006]), to the Bolivarian socialism of Venezuela's Hugo Chavez, to the grassroots populism of Bolivia's Evo Morales, much of the region is moving away from a U.S. brand of democracy where economic and political elites dominate the policy-making spaces of government.

President [George W.] Bush witnessed this firsthand in November 2005 when he attended the Fourth Summit of the Americas in Argentina. He was greeted by tens of thousands of protesters decrying the U.S. war in Iraq, the U.S. practice and defense of torture, and above all else, U.S. prescriptions for trade policy through the so-called Free Trade Area of the Americas (FTAA). While the Bush administration maintains that the majority of regional governments still support the U.S.-promoted FTAA, the largest and most powerful nations of South America are increasingly joining forces to support an intra-regional model of trade known as Mercosur. Rather than expanding the NAFTA trade model to the entire hemisphere, as the FTAA would most likely do, Mercosur has prioritized trade amongst South American nations, building an ever-stronger block of countries which can negotiate more forcefully with the United States.

Corruption and Human Rights Violations

Along with the perennial challenges of economic and social exclusion, human rights violations by security forces, widespread corruption, and weak and ineffective institutions of government, the region faces a myriad of other human rights challenges, some of which are merely new manifestations of unresolved old conflicts. Organized crime is having a profoundly corrosive and debilitating effect on many Latin America countries. No longer limited to drug cartels, organized crime now extends into areas such as arms trafficking, trafficking in stolen autos, and even human trafficking—including phony adoptions. These rackets are increasingly powerful where they are infiltrated by retired military officers who continue to wield considerable strength within government. Organized crime's impact on government and society is reaching or has reached crisis proportions in Colombia, Guatemala, Haiti, Mexico, and elsewhere.

The rights of women and minority populations are receiving renewed attention in the region. Violence against women—including formerly tolerated practices including intrafamily violence, sexual violence, and murders of young women—is for the first time receiving widespread public scrutiny. The many young women murdered in northern Mexico and Guatemala have brought to light the ugly fact that women, especially poor women, are broadly viewed as expendable, with police and justice officials barely lifting a finger to stop, much less investigate or bring to justice, those responsible for such heinous crimes. Only through the efforts of family members, victims associations, and human rights groups have these profound injustices come to light.

Likewise, people of indigenous and African descent are slowly gaining new acceptance and political power throughout the region. This is less due to benevolent governments than to new social movements demanding that their rights be taken seriously—and in some cases taking control of the institutions of government. From the Zapatista movement in Mexico, to Afro-Colombians, to the federations of indigenous peoples in Ecuador, Peru, and Bolivia, historically marginalized and oppressed peoples are demanding respect for their basic rights as human beings: traditional land rights and cultural identity, equality before the law, and a say in decision-making about the nation's future, including use of natural resources.

The Challenges Ahead

Enormous challenges lie ahead for the new social movements and civil society, but they may be the best hope for tackling the region's persistent and age-old problems, which threaten once again to plunge the region into open social conflict punctuated by authoritarianism and repression. If meaningful change is to come to the region, it will need to come through a grassroots democracy that has been largely absent.

The United States has a poor track record of dealing constructively with these social movements, suggesting that at best we can demand that the United States not obstruct these developments by vilifying the new leaders and insisting on its own narrow self-interests. What Latin America needs now more than ever is a neighbor to the North that respects the new voices in the region and supports economic and social policies that benefit the poor, reduce inequality, and strengthen civilian institutions. That kind of change could truly help to usher in a new era for a long-beleaguered hemisphere.

> *"The return to civilian, constitutionally elected governments [has] seen an end to the pattern of widespread and systematic enforced disappearances, extrajudicial executions and torture of political opponents."*

Human Rights Advocacy Is Expanding in Latin America

Amnesty International

In the following viewpoint, Amnesty International claims that while much remains to be done, Latin America is taking steps to improve human rights in the region. Most Latin American constitutions guarantee fundamental rights, and most nations have ratified key international human rights treaties, the authors maintain. The region also continues to take steps to reduce violence against women, the authors assert. Pressure on Latin American governments to address economic and social inequality will promote continued improvements in the status of human rights in Latin America, the authors reason. Amnesty International is a human rights advocacy organization.

Amnesty International, "Americas," *Amnesty International Report 2008: The State of the World's Human Rights*, New York, NY: Amnesty International, 2008. Copyright © 2008 Amnesty International Publications, 1 Easton Street, London WC1X 0DW, United Kingdom. www.amnesty.org. All rights reserved. Reproduced by permission.

As you read, consider the following questions:

1. According to Amnesty International, what nation has not ratified key international human rights treaties?

2. In what way is gender discrimination in Latin America often compounded, in the authors' view?

3. How have communities in Mexico and in several South Andean countries continued to campaign for the realization of their rights, in the authors' opinion?

If human rights are today at the heart of the UN [United Nations] project, it is in large part thanks to the efforts of Latin American countries. Human rights ranked low in the list of priorities for the major post-war powers involved in drafting the UN Charter, including the USA. However, in 1945, just before the San Francisco UN founding meeting, the Inter-American Conference met in Mexico City and decided to seek the inclusion of a transnational declaration of rights in the UN Charter which eventually led to the adoption of the Universal Declaration of Human Rights [UDHR]. In May 1948, several months before the adoption of the UDHR, the Inter-American Conference adopted the American Declaration of the Rights and Duties of Man, the world's first general human rights instrument.

A Crucial Contribution

This crucial contribution to international human rights has been overshadowed in the intervening years by the military rule which dominated much of the region. From the 1960s to the mid-1980s many Latin American countries endured years of military government characterized by widespread and systematic human rights violations. Some violations, such as enforced disappearances, became emblematic of both the regimes and of Amnesty International's campaigning focus in the region during those years.

The end of military rule and the return to civilian, constitutionally elected governments have seen an end to the pattern of widespread and systematic enforced disappearances, extrajudicial executions and torture of political opponents. However, the hopes that a new era of respect for human rights had arrived have in many cases proved unfounded.

Most constitutions guarantee fundamental rights and most countries in the region have ratified key international human rights treaties. A notable exception to the latter is the USA, one of only two countries in the world not to have ratified the UN Convention on the Rights of the Child and one of only a handful of countries not to have ratified the UN Women's Convention. The US government has also informed the UN of its intention not to ratify the Rome Statute of the International Criminal Court.

Lingering Weaknesses

The legacy of the authoritarian regimes of the past lives on in the institutional weaknesses which continue to bedevil many Latin American countries, particularly in Central America, and in the Caribbean. Corruption, the absence of judicial independence, impunity for state officials, and weak governments have undermined confidence in state institutions. Equal protection may exist in law, but it is often denied in practice, particularly for those in disadvantaged communities.

The gulf that remains between law and practice in many countries in the region has its origins in the historical abuse of law enforcement which successive governments have failed to address. Police and security forces and justice systems have long been used to repress dissent and to sustain corruption and entrenched economic and political interests. This abuse of power persists. The vast majority of those punished or imprisoned by justice systems are powerless and underprivileged. Those responsible for abuses of power and human rights frequently remain unpunished.

Although abusive practices have remained largely unchanged, the rationale for them has shifted. The techniques previously used to repress political dissent, have now been turned on those challenging social injustice and discrimination—such as human rights defenders—and those they seek to support.

A whole range of rights is being championed by these rights defenders in the context of vibrant and increasingly self-confident social movements across the region. A wide variety of organizations, far from the thoughts and experiences of those who adopted the UDHR 60 years ago, are taking forward the continuing struggle to ensure the rights it guaranteed become a reality. . . .

Conflict in Colombia

Civilians continued to bear the brunt of Colombia's long-running internal armed conflict. Although the number of those killed or kidnapped continued to fall, all parties to the conflict—the security forces, paramilitaries and guerrilla groups—continued to commit serious human rights abuses. Hundreds of thousands of people were again displaced by confrontations between the warring parties. . . .

Stamping Out Violence Against Women

Latin America continued to take important and innovative steps to stamp out violence against women and make gender equality a reality. Mexico and Venezuela, for example, passed new laws to combat violence against women. These laws broaden the definition of violence against women and provide a more comprehensive framework of protection mechanisms. Some initiatives to tackle violence against women—for example the pioneering women's police stations in Brazil—continued to be hampered by a lack of adequate resources and continuing misconceptions about the nature and extent of the problem. In the USA, following concerted campaigning by a wide coalition of groups, Congress recommended increased funding to implement the Violence Against Women Act, a federal law providing a range of measures at state and local levels.

Most of those responsible for violence against women were not held to account, reflecting a continuing lack of political will to address the problem. Many of the difficulties faced by women seeking justice were replicated from country to country. Amnesty International's research consistently revealed a lack of shelters providing appropriate protection; poor training of law enforcement officials in appropriate investigation techniques, including forensic examinations; and prosecution processes that did not address the needs of women for protection and ensure women's rights and dignity were promoted. Those women who did manage to get their cases as far as prosecution often faced discriminatory attitudes from the criminal justice system and further intimidation from their abusers.

Gender discrimination was often compounded by other forms of discrimination. If a woman is black, Indigenous, lesbian or poor, she will often face even greater barriers in getting justice. And if abusers know that they can beat, rape and kill women with impunity, then these abuses become both more widespread and more entrenched. For example, Native American and Alaska Native women in the USA who experience sexual violence are regularly met with inaction or indifference. They also experience disproportionately high levels of rape and sexual violence; US Justice Department figures have indicated that American Indian and Alaska Native women are some 2.5 times more likely to be raped or sexually assaulted than women in the USA in general. In Canada, government statistics demonstrate that Indigenous women are five times more likely than other women to die from violence, highlighting the desperate need for a comprehensive national action plan to address the violence and protect Indigenous women from discrimination.

Justice and Impunity

In April [2007], a federal court of appeals in Buenos Aires, Argentina, ruled that pardons granted to former military ruler Jorge Videla and former Admiral Emilio Massera in 1989 for crimes under international law were unconstitutional and therefore null and void.

In September [2007], the Chilean Supreme Court of Justice delivered a historic decision when it approved the extradition of former Peruvian President Alberto Fujimori to face charges of corruption and human rights abuses in Peru.

However, in November [2007] the Chilean Supreme Court acquitted a retired colonel of the enforced disappearance of three people in 1973 on the basis that the statute of limitations had expired. This judgment flouted international human rights standards and was a setback for all those seeking justice and redress for crimes committed under the military government of former President Augusto Pinochet. The Supreme Court of Panama also ruled that enforced disappearances committed in the late 1960s and early 1970s by state agents were covered by the statute of limitations.

Amnesty laws remained in place in Chile and Uruguay for crimes committed during the military governments of the 1970s and 1980s. However, in Uruguay the appeals court confirmed in September [2007] the trial and detention of former President Juan Maria Bordaberry (1971–1976) as co-author of 10 homicides. In December [2007], former President General Gregorio Alvarez (1981–1985) was arrested and charged as co-author of the enforced disappearances of more than 30 people.

Crimes by Agents of the State

In Mexico a federal judge concluded in July [2007] that the massacre of students in Tlatelolco square in 1968 constituted a crime of genocide, but that there was insufficient evidence against former President Luis Echeverria to continue the prosecution.

Human rights violations committed by agents of the state continued to be poorly investigated in most countries. In Brazil, El Salvador, Guatemala, Haiti and Jamaica, for example, human rights violations committed by law enforcement officials were rarely, if ever, prosecuted.

Corruption, inefficiency and lack of clear political will to bring those responsible for human rights violations to account characterized justice systems in many parts of the region. In addition the use of military and police courts to try personnel who commit human rights violations remained a serious concern. In Colombia, for example, many of the more than 200 killings by the security forces reported in 2007 were referred to the military justice system where the military's assertion that the victims were killed in combat was usually accepted and the cases closed without further scrutiny. In Mexico, the National Human Rights Commission found that military personnel were responsible for committing serious abuses against a number of civilians while participating in policing operations. Despite the consistent failure of military courts to ensure justice in human rights cases, the Commission failed to recommend that such cases be tried in civilian courts.

In the context of US conduct in the "war on terror", a lack of accountability for human rights violations remains a serious problem, particularly at higher levels in the chain of command.

Universal Jurisdiction

In Argentina and Panama new legislation was introduced providing for universal jurisdiction. In December [2007] President [George W.] Bush signed into law the US Genocide Accountability Act of 2007, which permits the investigation and prosecution of genocide if the alleged offender is brought into, or found in, the USA, even if the crime occurred outside the country.

Freedom in the Americas

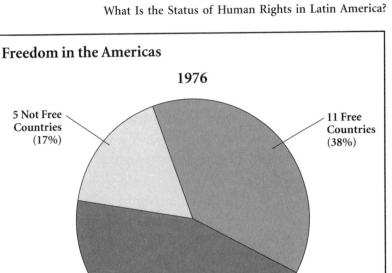

1976

5 Not Free
Countries
(17%)

11 Free
Countries
(38%)

13 Partly Free
Countries
(45%)

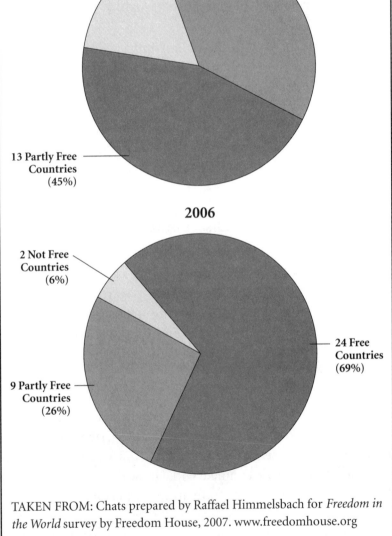

2006

2 Not Free
Countries
(6%)

24 Free
Countries
(69%)

9 Partly Free
Countries
(26%)

TAKEN FROM: Chats prepared by Raffael Himmelsbach for *Freedom in the World* survey by Freedom House, 2007. www.freedomhouse.org

There was no substantial progress in the cases against former President General José Efraín Ríos Montt and other high-ranking former officers in the Guatemalan military. A ruling by the Constitutional Court, preventing the implementation of warrants for General Ríos Montt's arrest and a request for his extradition issued by a Spanish judge in 2006, was widely criticized for failing to recognize the principle of universal jurisdiction.

In December [2007], an Italian judge issued arrest warrants for 146 former military and political officials from Argentina, Bolivia, Brazil, Chile, Paraguay, Peru and Uruguay. The arrests related to the killing and enforced disappearance of South American citizens of Italian origin during Operation Condor, a joint plan agreed between at least six military governments in the 1970s and 1980s to eliminate political opponents.

Economic and Social Discrimination

Pressure mounted on new Latin American and Caribbean governments to fulfill their promises to address deep-rooted economic and social inequalities. Some poverty reduction programmes were recognized as having a positive impact, but others were criticized for their emphasis on charity rather than on the realization of human rights and the promotion of equality.

The persistent political exclusion of large sections of the population, particularly Afro-descendants and Indigenous Peoples, was linked to discrimination and barriers to accessing a whole range of services essential for the realization of human rights. This was coupled with a continuing tendency to treat large sectors of the population as peripheral or to exclude them when defining economic development. A lack of transparency and accountability frequently served to protect vested economic interests and remained a major obstacle to overcoming poverty and discrimination.

However, communities continued to organize to campaign for the realization of their rights, often in the face of threats and intimidation. In Mexico, for example, large numbers of members of Indigenous and peasant communities opposed projects such as the construction of a dam at La Parota. In several South Andean countries, communities organized to oppose mineral extraction activities which threatened to encroach on protected lands or to cause serious environmental damage.

> "Bringing military officers to justice for human rights violations committed under dictatorships in the 1970s and 1980s has been a slow process."

Bringing Human Rights Violators to Justice in Latin America Is Difficult

Barbara J. Fraser

In the following viewpoint, Barbara J. Fraser asserts that although Latin American courts have begun to pursue cases that will bring those who violate human rights to justice, advocates pursuing these cases are coming under increasing attack. In Peru, for example, she maintains that lawyers, witnesses, and victims are being harassed. Indeed, Fraser claims, social protest in Latin America is increasingly seen as a crime. Conflation of protest with terrorism further complicates attempts to pursue officials who violate human rights, she adds. Fraser writes for the Catholic News Service.

Barbara J. Fraser, "As Human Rights Cases Go to Court, Latin Americans Come Under Attack," *Catholic News Service*, July 1, 2008. Reproduced by permission.

As you read, consider the following questions:

1. What does Fraser say is making it difficult to assign responsibility for the murder of one hundred peasant farmers in the southern highlands of Ayacucho, Peru?

2. According to the author, how many babies did human rights groups estimate were taken from parents who were political opponents during Argentina's "dirty war"?

3. Why did several Brazilian bishops receive death threats, according to an April 2008 bishops' conference report cited by Fraser?

Unprecedented human rights cases are moving through the courts in countries such as Peru, Argentina and Chile, raising hopes that perpetrators will be brought to justice. But human rights workers continue to come under attack.

Attacks on Human Rights Workers

The apparently contradictory combination is not a coincidence.

"There's a connection between progress in cases against high-level officials and attacks against human rights workers involved in those cases," Coletta Youngers, a senior fellow with the nonprofit Washington Office on Latin America, told *Catholic News Service* [CNS].

In Peru, where former President Alberto Fujimori is on trial in connection with two high-profile cases of killings by a death squad that occurred while he was in office, the Pro Human Rights Association, known by its Spanish acronym APRODEH, has suffered harassment and the theft of computers and documents.

On June 10 [2008], police and busloads of unidentified protesters—some of whom admitted to APRODEH staff members that they were paid to participate—demonstrated outside the organization's offices, and an anonymous e-mail attacking APRODEH lawyer Francisco Soberon has been circulating in Lima.

Seventy-five attacks on lawyers, witnesses and victims involved in human rights cases have been reported in Peru since 2006. Soberon said the incidents reflect how difficult it is for Peruvians to come to grips with the political violence that racked the country between 1980 and 2000, and the impunity that has allowed many perpetrators of human rights violations to remain free.

In the southern highlands of Ayacucho, which was the epicenter of the violence, a team of forensic anthropologists is excavating a mass grave site where witnesses say soldiers killed more than 100 peasant farmers. Peruvian army officials have said they cannot tell who was responsible because personnel records were destroyed.

That stymies the investigation, "because if we don't have the names of the perpetrators, the case cannot go forward," said Ronald Gamarra, executive secretary of the National Human Rights Coordinating Committee, an umbrella committee of Peruvian human rights organizations that includes many church groups.

"There is little political support (for investigations), and therefore there is no pressure for the cases to move ahead," he said.

A Slow Process

Bringing military officers to justice for human rights violations committed under dictatorships in the 1970s and 1980s has been a slow process. In Chile, about 600 people, most of them former military personnel, are being tried for crimes dating back to the dictatorship of Gen. Augusto Pinochet. About 100 have been sentenced, but human rights groups have criticized the government for the sluggish proceedings.

In Argentina, where cases related to the 1976–1983 "dirty war" also are making their way through the courts, three military officers were found dead under suspicious circumstances between December 2007 and February 2008. All were defendants in human rights cases.

Former Lt. Col. Paul Alberto Navone was found dead in February [2008], just days before he was due to testify in a case involving the 1978 theft of newborn twins from a woman who had been arrested. Human rights groups estimate that about 200 babies were taken from their parents and given away. In most cases, the biological parents were political opponents who were then killed.

In Guatemala, a study published [in 2007] reported a steady increase in attacks on people involved in prosecuting human rights cases. The number rose from 127 in 2004 to 224 in 2005 and 278 in 2006, with more than 150 attacks reported in the first eight months of 2007.

"It is a very delicate situation," said Nery Rodenas, a lawyer and the director of the Archbishop's Human Rights Office in Guatemala City, in a telephone interview with CNS.

Finding Little Protection

Attacks target not only human rights activists, but also community leaders in remote parts of the country who have little protection, Rodenas said.

And, as in Peru, there is often an increase in such attacks when a high-profile case finally goes to trial.

Rodenas blamed what he called "clandestine groups" for many of the attacks. Some of those groups date back to before the 36-year civil war that ended in 1996, but they gained strength during those decades, he said.

The groups apparently have ties to the government and organized crime, according to a report released [in 2007] by Human Rights Watch.

A Culture of Impunity

A culture of impunity is still the norm throughout much of the Americas. In many cases impunity exists for crimes of torture and ill-treatment, "disappearances" and extrajudicial executions; in other cases, the crimes committed by non-state actors are simply not investigated. Similarly, there is widespread impunity for crimes committed against women and girls, especially domestic and sexual violence.

Andrew Thompson,
"Democracy and Human Rights in the Americas,"
Igloo Expert Blog: Human Rights and
International Governance, August 29, 2007.
www.trudeaufoundation.ca/thompsonhrblog/democrac.

"The Guatemalan justice system, which has little ability even to contain common crime, has so far proven no match for this powerful and dangerous threat to the rule of law," the report said.

In Brazil, the bishops' conference in April [2008] issued a statement of support for Bishop Erwin Krautler of Xingu, Bishop Jose Azcona Hermoso of Marajo and Bishop Flavio Giovenale of Abaetetuba. The bishops had received death threats for speaking out against slave labor and the sexual exploitation of children, and in favor of peasant farmers' land rights.

Those cases are tied to what Soberon sees as a growing tendency throughout the region for governments to view social protests as criminal acts.

Government officials in some countries, including Peru and Ecuador, have gone so far as to suggest that those protest ers are infiltrated by terrorists. As a result, there is less public opposition to threats against the demonstrators or a police crackdown on the protests.

"My general sense is that in Latin America, after a period of stagnation, we are beginning to see progress amid the difficulties" in cases of human rights violations stemming from civil wars and dictatorships, Soberon said.

The new trend, however, bears watching.

"There is no country in Latin America that is not affected by government efforts to criminalize protest and to equate protest with terrorism," he said.

> "While human rights groups caution that many countries still have a long way to go to end high-level impunity, the tide does seem to be turning."

Efforts to Bring Human Rights Violators to Justice in Latin America Are Improving

Isabel Vincent

In the following viewpoint, Isabel Vincent argues that the tide is turning in efforts to pursue human rights violators in Latin America. High-level officials, such as former Peruvian President Alberto Fujimori, are facing trial for corruption and political murders, she asserts. In fact, Vincent claims, even in countries such as Argentina, in which civilian governments declared amnesty for human rights violators, courts have ruled such proclamations unconstitutional, clearing the way for prosecutions. According to the author, more Latin American leaders have concluded that none of its citizens is above the law. Vincent is a journalist and author.

Isabel Vincent, "Go Directly to Jail: Impunity May Finally Become a Thing of the Past in Latin America," *Maclean's*, vol. 120, November 26, 2007, p. 40. Reproduced by permission of the author.

As you read, consider the following questions:

1. What happened in Santiago, Chile, that signaled a sea change in Latin America, in Vincent's opinion?

2. For what crime was Frederico Von Wernich, a Catholic priest, convicted, according to the author?

3. What was the most telling episode in the battle to end impunity in Chile, according to Vincent?

When police in the Chilean capital of Santiago rounded up the family and closest associates of former dictator Augusto Pinochet [in October 2007] on corruption charges and briefly stuck them in jail, Latin Americans could hardly believe it. Although most of the charges were later dropped, the arrests seemed to signal a sea change in the region. For years, Latin America has allowed leaders and their friends to get away with robbery and murder. Was impunity finally dead in Chile, where the military government participated in the deaths of thousands in the 1970s and 1980s, and is accused of stealing millions of dollars?

Turning the Tide

While human rights groups caution that many countries still have a long way to go to end high-level impunity, the tide does seem to be turning. Two weeks before the Chilean arrests, Peru's Supreme Court ordered the extradition of former president Alberto Fujimori, who has spent seven years in self-imposed exile. Fujimori, now in a Peruvian jail, will face trial on charges of corruption and human rights abuses.

Similarly in Brazil, the Supreme Court ruled in August [2007] that a former chief of staff to President Luis Inácio Lula da Silva would stand trial for his alleged involvement in one of the biggest corruption scandals in recent history. José Dirceu is accused of being involved in an illegal fundraising scheme. Prosecutors say that public and private funds were diverted into the "mensalao" or "big monthly payoff" scandal during Lula's first term in order to obtain political favours.

Argentina was recently gripped by the three-month trial of Christian Frederico Von Wernich, 69, a Catholic priest. He was convicted for his involvement in seven murders, 42 abductions and 31 cases of torture during the so-called Dirty War against leftists between 1976 and 1983, which saw the disappearance and deaths of an estimated 30,000 people. Von Wernich worked as the chaplain to the Buenos Aires provincial police, telling police torturers that they were doing God's work, and passing on information from detainees after gaining their trust. He is only the third person to be convicted of human rights abuses in the country; after military rule ended in Argentina in 1983, the civilian governments proclaimed a general amnesty, which was finally ruled unconstitutional in 2003, opening the way for prosecution on human rights violations. "The importance of [the Von Wernich] case is fundamental because it's judging the participation of civilians in the military dictatorship, and not just any civilian but a member of the Catholic Church," said one of the prosecutors.

The Pursuit of Pinochet

But perhaps the most telling episode in the battle to end impunity came as police in Chile arrested Pinochet's 84-year-old widow, his five adult children, and his secretary and accountant along with several others, for their alleged role in misusing public funds. Prosecutors claim they participated in a scheme to help the ex-dictator stash away some $26 million in foreign banks. Prosecutor Teresa Muñoz said Pinochet's widow, Lucia Hiriart, and one of his sons, had access to accounts that the general used to conceal money. Before his death of a heart attack [in December 2006], Pinochet had been facing charges of tax evasion, forgery of official documents, and numerous human rights abuses committed during his 17 years in power.

"Pinochet to Face Justice," cartoon by Patrick Chappatte, *The International Herald Tribune*. Copyright © 2004 by Patrick Chappatte and CagleCartoons.com. All rights reserved.

The Pinochet family has repeatedly denied the accusations, saying that Pinochet's funds were legally accumulated from savings, investments and donations he received. At the end of October [2007], a Chilean appeals court seemed to agree, and dropped charges against Pinochet's widow, four of his children, and 10 of the general's closest associates. However, indictments against Pinochet's eldest son Augusto, 62, and two of his former associates were upheld.

The family has long maintained that the indictments were politically motivated. But in August 2004, an investigation by the U.S. Senate found 125 secret bank accounts belonging to Pinochet and his family in the Riggs Bank, headquartered in

Washington, and in banks in Europe and the Caribbean. The Riggs Bank was sold in 2005; the Pinochet funds were transferred to other foreign banks and then reinvested in real estate. Now, regardless of the charges being dropped, the fact that Pinochet family members spent two days in jail underscores Chilean President Michelle Bachelet's declaration when the arrests were announced: "Nobody is above the law." Bachelet could just as well have been referring to the entire region—and Latin American prosecutors and human rights activists are hoping she's right.

> *"In spite of the efforts being made, 'we are still in debt to the indigenous peoples,' says Leon. 'We are in debt to societies, and we are facing situations that limit even the practice of democracy.'"*

Progress for the Rights of Indigenous People in Latin America Has Been Slow

Amparo Trujillo

In the following viewpoint, Amparo Trujillo notes the slow progress towards the "realization of the recognition of the rights of indigenous peoples." According to Trujillo, Ambassador Juan Leon Alvarado, Alternative Representative of the Guatemalan Mission to the Organization of the Americas (OAS), member states of the OAS "do not have a clear vision" of what the contents of the Declaration on the Rights of Indigenous Peoples should be. Trujillo adds that Leon believes that some governments fear "the declaration might contradict national and international legislation." Leon adds that "negotiations have yet to include topics related to the respect for indigenous peoples' forms of organization, their aspirations, and their fully recognized

Amparo Trujillo, "Raising Awareness, Reaffirming Rights," translated by Kathy A. Ogle, *Americas* (English Edition), vol. 58, no. 6, November–December 2006.

rights." However, although poverty is severe among indigenous peoples and indigenous women have long been discriminated against "for being women and for being indigenous," the OAS is committed to reducing the poverty and ending the discrimination. Amparo Trujillo is an information specialist in the OAS Department of Press and Communications.

As you read, consider the following questions:

1. According to Leon, what does the concept of "self-determination" mean to indigenous peoples?
2. How do poverty rates among indigenous peoples compare to rates among the general populations of Latin America?
3. What actions by the International Labor Organization and the United Nations may help to promote the rights of indigenous peoples?

No one would argue that the indigenous peoples of the Americas shouldn't enjoy the same rights and opportunities as all citizens; but neither would anyone claim that the goal has been reached. Gaining full recognition of the rights of indigenous peoples has been a slow process. In the Organization of American States (OAS), negotiations on the American Declaration on the Rights of Indigenous Peoples have been going on for seven years, and a similar process in the United Nations has lasted even longer.

This does not mean that the effort has been a waste of time, however, says Ambassador Juan Leon Alvarado, Alternate Representative of the Guatemalan Mission to the OAS. For the last two years, Leon has presided over the working group in charge of the negotiations. "The discussions have generated initiatives," he says, "and they've raised the awareness of societies and governments. I think that's something we have to remember."

Leon, who belongs to the Maya K'iche people of Guatemala, says that the delegations of the thirty-four OAS member countries still do not have a clear vision about what the final content of the declaration should be. "Some believe that we have to invent the rights of indigenous peoples from scratch; others believe that it's not necessary to confer rights; others have the idea that indigenous people don't think and don't have their own values and that therefore we need to make a document that turns them into dependents of the state, in other words to reform the chain of oppression and limitations that already exist to the detriment of indigenous peoples' rights."

Leon believes that the American Declaration should reflect and reaffirm natural rights that should already be in effect and fully practiced and that there is no need to invent anything: "These rights are exercised and have been exercised for thousands of years."

One of the challenges, according to Leon, is to overcome the fear that arises within some governments that the declaration might contradict national and international legislation. Concerns tend to emerge about complex concepts like "self-determination." From the point of view of the indigenous peoples, Leon explains, this concept does not refer to the creation of independent states, but rather the absolute freedom to make decisions about the design, management, and execution of plans, strategies, and programs that have to do with all of their political, economic, and social rights. "If that's how self-determination is understood, then what is there to be afraid of?" Leon asks.

In November 2005, at Mar del Plata, Argentina, heads of state and government leaders convening for the last Summit of the Americas made this commitment in the Declaration and Action Plan, advocating "for a prompt and successful conclusion of negotiations" on the OAS American Declaration project.

It was sixteen years earlier, in 1989, that the OAS General Assembly charged the Inter-American Commission on Human

Rights (IACHR) with preparing a legal instrument related to the rights of indigenous peoples, then, in 1999, it established a working group of the Permanent Council to consider the American Declaration project. Since then, the group has met seven times; five times in Washington, once in Guatemala, and most recently in Brazil. The governments of Bolivia, Mexico, and Venezuela have offered to host the talks next year, by which time the working group hopes that more progress will have been made on fundamental aspects of the project—such as cultural identity; political and organizational rights; social, economic, and property rights; and general provisions.

The OAS negotiation process includes representatives of indigenous peoples from all over the continent, with participation financed through contributions from the governments of Brazil, Canada, Finland, Italy, Nicaragua, and the United States.

In spite of the efforts being made, "we are still in debt to the indigenous peoples," says Leon. "We are in debt to societies, and we are facing situations that limit even the practice of democracy." He adds that although there has been progress in other aspects, the negotiations have yet to include topics related to the respect for indigenous peoples' forms of organization, their aspirations, and their fully recognized rights.

One of the priorities of OAS member states is to fight extreme poverty in the region, where the native population is one of the most vulnerable groups. A study published by the World Bank concludes that indigenous people—some 45 million people in the Americas, members of more than four hundred indigenous groups—who comprise 10 percent of the Latin American population, are the most disadvantaged group. "While the poverty rate is high in Latin America in general, it is particularly severe and deep among the indigenous peoples," says Gillette Hall, World Bank economist and co-author of the study. Harry Patrinos, also a World Bank economist and study co-author, adds, "Poverty rates among the indigenous popula-

Rights Denied, Distorted or Diminished

Some of the main rights and liberties [of indigenous peoples] that have been denied, distorted or diminished (although the claims are urgent) include:

- recognition by States of the physical and cultural existence of indigenous peoples;

- the right to the real and effective ownership of traditional lands and territories and to the resources (both material and spiritual) that they contain;

- the right of indigenous peoples to have their own understanding of their history;

- the right to participate in and propose policies and projects for development, health, education and other areas;

- the right to have effective mechanisms to protest against or oppose legislation, administrative measures, projects, policies and programmes that have a negative impact on the life, economy or environment of their communities;

- the real and effective recognition of indigenous legal systems and religions, and the contributions that indigenous cultures have made to the progress of humanity, especially in relation to the environment, agriculture, philosophy, mathematics and other fields.

Jose Francisco Cali Tzay,
"Discrimination Against Indigenous Peoples:
The Latin American Context,"
UN Chronicle, September 2007.

tion are higher and fall more slowly, which is particularly bad news for a continent that has set its sights on meeting the Millennium Development Goal of halving poverty by 2015."

The World Bank study analyzes poverty rates in four countries of the region that have high indigenous populations: "In Bolivia and Guatemala, for example, more than half of the total population is poor, but almost three-quarters of the indigenous population is poor. Poverty among indigenous people in Ecuador is about 87 percent and reaches 96 percent in the rural highlands. In Mexico, the incidence of extreme poverty in 2002 was 4.5 times higher in predominantly indigenous municipalities than in nonindigenous municipalities, up from a ratio of 3.7 times a decade earlier. Of all poor households in Peru, 43 percent are indigenous."

Among indigenous peoples, women are especially marginalized, says Ambassador Leon. "Indigenous women of the Americas have suffered double discrimination historically for being women and for being indigenous, in addition to being discriminated against inside their own communities."

At the OA[S] meeting in Brasilia last March, the working group unanimously approved an article recognizing the state's responsibility for the full realization of women's rights and the prevention of violence and discrimination of all kinds. Speaking at the meeting, OAS Assistant Secretary General Albert Ramdin said that "it is clear that our countries cannot attain desired levels of development, stability, and democracy when a significant percentage of the population is deprived of real opportunities that will enable them to reach their full potential."

In 1989, the International Labor Organization (ILO) adopted Convention 169, the only legal instrument recognized internationally that protects the indigenous population, estimated at 350 million people worldwide. This legal instrument includes aspects such as land rights, access to natural resources, health, education, professional training, working conditions, and cross-border contacts. To date, the ILO convention has been ratified by seventeen countries, including thirteen OAS member states: Argentina, Bolivia, Brazil, Colombia, Costa Rica, Dominica, Ecuador, Guatemala, Honduras, Mexico, Paraguay, Peru, and Venezuela.

On June 29, the United Nations Human Rights Council passed the Universal Declaration of Indigenous Peoples, which had been debated for twenty years. The declaration recognizes self-determination, establishes that indigenous peoples should be allowed to exploit the natural resources on their lands, and limits military activity in their territories. In addition, it recognizes the collective rights of indigenous peoples, such as the right to preserve their cultural values and ethinic identity, and protection from any effort to expel them from their ancestral lands.

The office of the Special Rapporteur for Indigenous Peoples' Rights of the OAS IACHR supports the UN's step, saying that this declaration "will enrich the debate in the OAS and will be considered a minimum standard for its reflections." This means that if, for example, the UN declaration recognizes the right to self-determination, the OAS must recognize it because it has already achieved great consensus internationally, explains Isabel Madariaga specialist from the IACHR Special Rapporteur's office. "What the United Nations passes has to be a good guide for discussion in the OAS. The regional body should take up the discussion using the UN language as a starting point," she says.

It is important to clarify that the UN Human Rights Council passed the Universal Declaration by vote and not by consensus and that it still must be adopted by the General Assembly. Meanwhile, the OAS working group will continue to observe this parallel process with great attention.

Progress has also been made at the national level in the region. Brazil, Colombia, and Ecuador have advanced in their legislation and other countries are working toward such ends, though some have encountered obstacles due to the limitations of their own constitutions, says Aria Pena Doig vice president of the OAS working group. The principles contained in the UN declaration can help governments "to modify and revise their laws and even their constitutions in favor of indigenous peoples," she says.

Pena believes that the general declaration of principles currently making its way through the UN will help to promote the more detailed document being drawn up by the OAS. "This is precisely what will allow us to make progress and that's why I believe that in two years we will have completed a Declaration of the Americas," she says.

"Throughout the 1990s the indigenous movement [in Ecuador] grew in political strength and influence."

The Political Power of Indigenous Groups in Latin America Is Growing

Luis Angel Saavedra

In the following viewpoint, Luis Angel Saavedra maintains that the indigenous people of Latin America have a history of bringing communities together. Indeed, he claims, the indigenous political movement in the region has gained strength over the past two decades. In 2002, for example, the movement won the presidential elections in Ecuador. However, these leaders face serious challenges, Saavedra asserts. Indigenous leaders must work with others in a historically corrupt system and deal with the complicated realities that face governments, he concludes. Saavedra is a writer and academic director of the Regional Foundation of Human Rights Advice in Quito, Ecuador.

As you read, consider the following questions:

1. What made it hard to accept Ecuador's multicultural reality, according to Saavedra?

Luis Angel Saavedra, "Growing from the Grassroots," *New Internationalist*, vol. 356, May 2003, pp. 27–28. Copyright © 2003 *New Internationalist Magazine*. Reproduced by permission.

2. According to Saavedra, how were indigenous political demands channeled prior to the 1990s?

3. How have Latin American landowners misunderstood the *minga* in the view of Rodrigo Collaguazo, whom Saavedra quotes in his article?

On 10 August 1979, after 10 years of military dictatorship, Jaime Roldós was sworn in as Ecuador's elected President. He made his first speech to the National Congress in Kichwa, the main indigenous language. Politicians and landowners never forgave him, despite the use of indigenous icons—such as Rumiñahui, who led the fiercest resistance against the Spanish conquest—for patriotic purposes. Roldós died in suspicious circumstances—an air crash—in May 1981.

In 1982 his successor, Oswaldo Hurtado, wore the presidential sash with words written in Shuar, another indigenous language, when he gave his end-of-year report to Congress—and faced a political trial for doing so.

Ingrained racism among the white élite made it hard to accept the country's multicultural reality. Anything 'Indian' was an insult, synonymous with slavery and ignorance: 'Indian shit', 'Indian porter', 'to play the Indian' (act stupid) are terms found in many editions of the Royal Academy of the Spanish Language Dictionary. They are still used to degrade the indigenous peoples of the South American continent, or Abya Yala as many now prefer to call it.

'I used to cry when I was called "Indian", as I wasn't raised as an indigenous person. As an adult I had to struggle to recover my own language and cultural heritage,' recalls José Yungán, a leader of the Confederation of Indigenous Nationalities of Ecuador (CONAIE).

The 1990 Uprising

In June 1990 the established political order was shocked out of its complacency when thousands of indigenous people held their first national uprising, including roadblocks throughout the Andes and a march in Quito, the seat of political power.

'1990 was not the beginning of a process, but rather the conclusion of a long and drawn-out first stage of their struggle for autonomy, identity and respect,' says sociologist Alejandro Moreano.

Until then, indigenous political demands had been channelled through established political parties and enlightened sections of different churches. They played an important role in guiding indigenous leaders and helping to form indigenous organizations, such as the Ecuadorian Federation of Indians (FEI), founded in the 1930s by the Communist Party, and the Shuar People's Federation, established with the help of missionaries in the Amazon.

The 1990 uprising was also a moment for the recovery of indigenous history. In the 1930s Dolores Cacuango founded four indigenous bilingual schools where children could write in their own language. She coined the legendary cry: 'We are like moorland grass that grows again after it has been uprooted, and from this grass we shall sow the world.'

Cacuango was a leader of the FEI, as was another Kichwa leader, Tránsito Amaguaña, who founded the first indigenous agricultural workers' union and led the first indigenous peasant strike in 1944. Now in her nineties, 'Mama Tránsito' still has the strength to browbeat younger leaders who don't fulfil their people's mandates.

A Growing Movement

Throughout the 1990s the indigenous movement grew in political strength and influence. For the first time other Ecuadorians began to learn directly from the actors themselves, not from those who had spoken on their behalf.

'They misrepresented our ways, they didn't understand our philosophy. "Solidarity, complementarity and reciprocity" is more than just a slogan—it's our economic system,' says

A Movement Is Sparked

In 2003, following U.S. desires, the Bolivian government sold rights to natural gas which was then headed to the market for Mexican and U.S. consumers. On Oct. 12, the 511-year anniversary of the landing of Columbus, Bolivian soldiers attacked Indian peasants in the Andean city of El Alto, the largest Indian city in Latin America. Hundreds were wounded and 65 died, but it sparked a nationwide movement of peasants, Indians, and workers that culminated in the siege of La Paz and forced [then] President Gonzales Sanchez de Lozado to flee to Miami.

John C. Mohawk, "Bolivia's Indians Confront Globalization,"
Indian Country Today, *August 25, 2004.*

Rodrigo Collaguazo, a leader of CONFEUNASC, the campesino social-security union. '*Ama shua, ama quilla, ama llulla* (don't steal, don't lie, don't be lazy) are our guiding principles.'

In economic terms, 'solidarity' means helping those who have less. 'Complementarity' assumes that production is both a common right and a duty, so that communities cover shortfalls and distribute surpluses. 'Reciprocity' equates to: 'Today for you, tomorrow for me.' These three principles underlie one of the Andean people's greatest strengths: the *minga*, communal work such as harvesting or building an irrigation system.

The *Minga*

'Landowners misunderstood the *minga*,' continues Collaguazo, 'they thought of it as free indigenous labour for them—but that's serfdom. *Minga* means working together and everyone knowing that they'll get help when they need it. That's reciprocity.'

Since 1990 the concept of the minga has been used to bring people from all communities together to change the country. The Pachakutik political movement was founded to contest the 1996 general election, when seven Pachakutik deputies were elected to Congress. The indigenous movement's real strength was shown in the ousting of two corrupt presidents: Abdala Bucaram in February 1997, and Jamil Mahuad in January 2000.

'Although we couldn't form an indigenous government in 2000, we established a precedent: indigenous people are a force capable of attaining political power,' says Salvador Quishpe, a recently elected Pachakutik deputy.

January and February 2001 witnessed one of the largest and most effective uprisings. It paralyzed many parts of the country and again filled Quito's streets with indigenous-led marches. This time their demands became those of that large majority of Ecuadorians: the rural and urban poor.

In 2002 the indigenous movement entered the Presidential and general elections. It supported Colonel Lucio Gutiérrez Borbúa who, against all expectations, won the presidency on a radical ticket. His meteoric and contradictory political career was launched by the key role he played in the impromptu alliance that overthrew Jamil Mahuad. Pachakutik, with its national and local community-based networks, delivered a large proportion of the rural vote that ensured the victory of Colonel Gutiérrez.

Since Gutiérrez assumed the Presidency the indigenous movement has been living through the most complicated moment in its history. Two indigenous leaders, Luis Macas and Nina Pacari, became Ministers, of Agriculture and Foreign Affairs respectively.

Luis Macas belongs to the Saraguro Andean people of southern Ecuador and is one of the key thinkers on the Left of the indigenous movement. He takes over a ministry historically known for catering to the big Andean landowners and the coastal agro-industrial exporters.

The Colonial Counts

Nina Pacari has her work cut out in the Ministry of Foreign Affairs. As Marco Antonio Rodríguez, of the Casa de la Cultura Ecuatoriana, explains: 'The Foreign Ministry is where the descendants of colonial counts and viscounts go. The fact that an indigenous person has arrived there as Minister will be a great shock. In the end, those with a complex about "purity" will just have to accept that this country is a diverse one.'

To see two of their foremost leaders in important government positions has generated expectations among the poor and marginalized of Ecuador's divided society. However, the initial economic measures of the new government have already begun to create concern about the real extent of political clout that Pachakutik and the indigenous movement have over Gutiérrez and his advisers.

The first worrying sign was the economic team, made up of people linked to the country's traditionally corrupt and inefficient banking system. Within a couple of weeks they had raised fuel prices and public-transport fares—measures that enabled Gutiérrez to borrow $500 million from the IMF [International Monetary Fund]. 'The IMF is not so inflexible or as hard as some believe,' Gutiérrez assured the international press during a visit to Washington DC. Back in Ecuador, Pachakutik leaders confessed to not having received details of the agreement.

After years of protest against any price hike in fuel and fares, indigenous leaders of Ecuador—like the Bolivarian movement in Venezuela and the PT Workers' Party in Brazil—now have to juggle with the contradictions facing them in government. They know their decisions could lose the movement legitimacy and the respect it has gained from years of hard, principled struggle. But they also know that this is an historic opportunity to make a change in favour of all of Latin America's poor and marginalized peoples.

"Child labor is so intractable a problem [in Latin America] because it is the direct result of poverty and unemployment."

Child Labor Is a Serious Problem in Latin America

Jack Silicon

In the following viewpoint, Jack Silicon argues that as many as 48 million children work in Latin America to help their families survive. Indeed, Silicon maintains, child labor is a direct result of poverty and unemployment in Latin America. To reduce child labor in the region and, in turn, increase economic growth, he asserts, Latin America, with U.S. support, should improve its schools and make education available to all children. Silicon is a Latin Trade columnist who writes under the moniker Silicon Jack.

As you read, consider the following questions:

1. According to Silicon, what model should Latin American countries follow when striving to give working children "back their childhood"?

Jack Silicon, "Clock Watchers: Working Kids Keep Poor Latin American Families Afloat, But at a Long-Term Cost for the Region," *Latin Trade*, vol. 14, January 2006, p. 20. Copyright © 2006 Freedom Magazines, Inc. Reproduced by permission.

2. What rights does Article 27 of the Convention on the Rights of the Child guarantee, in the author's opinion?

3. How should Latin American governments raise school attendance, according to Silicon?

Until [2005], the gold mines ringing the Peruvian village of Santa Filomena employed hundreds of children as young as six years old. The young workers often inhaled toxic mercury used to extract gold. Today, all those children are in school. Officials are proudly calling the village high in the Andes their nation's first mining town free of child labor.

Credit for this humane achievement belongs to a project co-sponsored by the U.N. [United Nations] International Labor Organization (ILO) and a local nongovernmental organization. Together they built schools and, more importantly, created jobs for parents who no longer need to rely on their children's hard work. It's an important model for other Latin American countries that should be striving to give working children back their childhood.

An Ubiquitous Problem

An estimated 300,000 children labor in mines in Latin America—mostly in Bolivia, Ecuador, Colombia and Peru. Of course, the mining industry, which covets youngsters for their ability to squeeze through narrow tunnels where adults can't fit, is not the only offender. The ILO estimates that 48 million children work in Latin America, half of them under the age of 14. U.N. statistics show 17% of kids ages five to 14 work. Brazil, Bolivia, Peru and Guatemala have the largest number of underage workers.

Indeed, child labor is ubiquitous in Latin America—in construction, prostitution, orange groves, sugar fields, brick making, markets, charcoal kilns and in households, most often girls serving long hours as domestic servants. Yet the average child worker is not a Dickensian tot toiling in a sweatshop but a child working alongside a parent on a farm or in the underground economy to help feed, shelter and clothe the family.

A Family's Survival

Several years ago I spent some time in Franca, a city with hundreds of shoe factories known as the child labor capital of Brazil. Many parents told me that their children's pay—no matter how meager—was vital to their family's survival. In fact, some even argued that they had a right to ask their children to help, and that laws should protect them.

But the law also guarantees universal education. And each nation should abide by Article 27 of the Convention on the Rights of the Child, which cites the right for children to be protected from any work likely to be hazardous or to interfere with that education.

Child labor is so intractable a problem because it is the direct result of poverty and unemployment. In Argentina, the number of working children quintupled to 1.5 million after the historic economic collapse of 2001 and 2002. Obviously, working kids will never be sent back to their classrooms without a sharp reduction in poverty.

Taking the Problem Seriously

Nevertheless, recent developments have given activists hope that regional governments are finally taking the issue seriously. In June [2005], the ILO signed an agreement with Brazil, Colombia, Ecuador, Nicaragua and Peru to end child labor in small-scale mining and quarries by 2015. The new Central American Free Trade Agreement includes a commitment to create a "child-labor-free zone" by the end of the decade. And 7.5 million Brazilian families and 5 million Mexican families now receive monthly government subsidies to keep their children in school.

Latin American governments must find ways to raise school attendance by not only paying stipends but by reduc-

Rigoberta Menchú's Story

According to UNICEF, 'Child domestic workers are the world's most forgotten children . . . they may well be the most vulnerable and exploited of all, as well as the most difficult to protect'. Child domestics' isolation can be almost total; in Peru, one study showed that nearly a third *never* leave the premises. Invisible and unprotected, child household workers are vulnerable to physical and sexual abuse at the hands of their employers, and are often treated in a subhuman fashion. In Guatemala, one twelve-year-old indigenous girl faced a humiliating first night, *'the mistress called me. The food they gave me was a few beans with some very hard tortillas. There was a dog in the house, a pretty, white, fat dog. When I saw the maid bring out the dog's food—bits of meat, rice, things that the family ate—that hurt me very much. I was lower than the animals in the house.'*

The girl was Rigoberta Menchú, who later went on to win the Nobel Peace Prize for her work in promoting equal rights for Guatemala's impoverished Indian majority.

Duncan Green, "Child Labour in Latin America,"
Catholic Agency for Overseas Development, May 2004.
www.cafod.org.uk.

ing the costs of school uniforms, supplies and transportation and doling out scholarships and remedial classes for those who need it.

"If child labor is to be reduced and eventually eliminated, schools must be improved dramatically," Marta Suplicy, the former mayor of Silo Paulo, recently told reporters. Improving school education "opens a window for poor children who otherwise do not see an alternative."

Most importantly, reform makes economic sense.

In September [2005], an ILO study on the benefits of eliminating child labor showed that if Latin America invested US$105 billion in the next 20 years in schools and subsidies to poor families to keep their children in school, the region would benefit economically by $235 billion as a result of a healthier and more educated population.

Compulsory public education did not stunt the advance of industrialization and economic growth in the United States and United Kingdom more than a century ago—it fueled it. Education is the surest path to an end to child labor, and it will lift millions out of poverty.

Periodical Bibliography

The following articles have been selected to supplement the diverse views presented in this chapter.

Christopher L. Brown and Alyssa Smith	"Lesson 5: Poverty, Human Rights, and Social Change," *Latin America in Transition* [Southern Center for International Studies], 2008.
Economist	"The Americas: Shaking a Thirst for Justice: Human Rights," April 14, 2007.
Los Angeles Times	"Oil and Power in Latin America," March 29, 2008.
Judith Morrison	"Race and Poverty in Latin America: Addressing the Development Needs of African Descendants," *UN Chronicle*, September 2007.
Heraldo Munoz	"A Special Partnership with the UN: A Latin American Perspective," *UN Chronicle*, March 2007.
Melissa Nobles	"The Myth of Latin American Multiracialism," *Daedalus*, Winter 2005.
Marifeli Pérez-Stable	"Education Is the Key," *Miami Herald*, March 27, 2008.
Susan H. Preston	"Bang for the Buck: Latin America's Healthcare Systems Are As Different as the Nations Themselves—But Some Are More Effective Than Others," *LatinFinance*, October 2006.
Andrew Thompson	"Democracy and Human Rights in the Americas," Igloo Expert Blog: Human Rights and International Governance, August 29, 2007.
Jose Francisco Cali Tzay	"Discrimination Against Indigenous Peoples: The Latin American Context," *UN Chronicle*, September 2007.

For Further Discussion

Chapter 1

1. Duncan Currie asserts that those Latin American nations that engage in the global marketplace are showing signs of economic growth. Ken Frankel does not dispute this claim but argues that one-size-fits-all policies do not acknowledge the economic differences among the nations of Latin America, and that not all nations can effectively compete globally. Which point of view do you find more persuasive? Explain.

2. Many of the authors in this chapter refer to U.S.-promoted neoliberal economic policies, also known as the Washington Consensus. Some argue that these policies have effectively improved Latin American economies. Others, particularly Christy Thornton, claim that these policies have failed. The authors in this chapter on both sides of the debate cite concrete evidence to support their views. Based on this evidence, what conclusions have you drawn concerning the success or failure of these policies? Explain, citing the viewpoints.

3. While Matías Vernengo believes that the resurgence of Latin American populism poses a threat to the region's economies, Javier Santiso sees populism as a pragmatic reaction to social and economic conditions and therefore not reflective of a return to the failed political and economic policies of Latin America's past. Citing the viewpoints, explain how each author connects populism to the success or failure of Latin American economies. Which view do you find more persuasive?

4. Of the various factors explored by the authors in this chapter, which do you believe most significantly impacts Latin American economies? Citing from the viewpoints, explain your answer.

Chapter 2

1. John Barham believes that democratic institutions have become stronger in Latin America. Fernando Henrique Cardoso, however, sees the growth of populism as a threat to these institutions. Identify the affiliations of these two authors. In what way do you think these affiliations influence each author's argument? Which argument do you find more persuasive? Citing the texts, explain.

2. William F. Jasper argues that Communism is on the rise in Latin America. Michael Shifter contends that equating the region's populist movement with Communism is unmerited. What kinds of evidence does each author use to support his claim? Which evidence do you find more persuasive? Explain, citing from the texts.

3. Jaime Daremblum argues that political pragmatism explains the rise of populism in Latin America. Greg Grandin asserts that failed U.S.-promoted economic policies better explain the rise of populist leaders in the region. What are the strengths and weaknesses of each perspective? Which viewpoint do you find more persuasive? Explain, citing from the texts.

Chapter 3

1. Jerry Haas supports the U.S. embargo of Cuba, arguing that if Cuba is to become truly democratic, change must come from within. Vicki Huddleston argues that fifty years of isolation has failed to bring about change in Cuba. In fact, she claims, as long as the people of Cuba are isolated, change from within is impossible. What rhe-

torical strategies does each author use to support his or her viewpoint? Which type of rhetoric do you find more persuasive? Explain.

2. James Hill argues that to prevent instability in Latin America, the United States should continue its war against narcoterrorism in the region. On the other hand, John Lindsay-Poland contends that the United States should reduce its military presence in Latin America because it causes resentment and even contributes to human rights violations in the region. Identify the evidence in each viewpoint. Which do you find more persuasive? Explain.

3. What commonalities in rhetoric, style, and type of evidence can be found among the viewpoints on each side of the debate over the role the United States should play in Latin America? Do any of the viewpoints suffer from logical fallacies? Explain, citing from the viewpoints.

4. Of the policies explored in this chapter, which do you think would be most effective? Citing from the viewpoint, explain your answer.

Chapter 4

1. What rhetorical strategies does Eric L. Olson use to support his claim that some nations in Latin America continue to violate human rights? Cite examples of each rhetorical strategy from the text of his viewpoint. Is one strategy more persuasive than another? Explain.

2. While Amnesty International and Isabel Vincent do not deny that there is much work to be done, they contend that Latin America is improving in its efforts to address human rights. Eric L. Olson and Barbara J. Fraser assert, however, that the region's governments continue to exploit the people and ignore the rule of law. What changes do Olson and Fraser suggest are necessary to improve human rights in Latin America? Does anything in the viewpoints of Amnesty International and Vincent indicate that these

changes are being implemented in some nations? Explain your answers, citing from the viewpoints.

3. Luis Angel Saavedra asserts that the indigenous political movement in Latin America is growing. What challenges does Saavedra contend indigenous leaders face? Which do you think will be the greatest challenge? Explain your reasoning, citing any relevant viewpoints in this and other chapters.

4. Of the strategies proposed within the viewpoints in this chapter, which do you believe would most effectively promote human rights in Latin America? Explain your answer citing from the viewpoints.

Organizations to Contact

The editors have compiled the following list of organizations concerned with the issues debated in this book. The descriptions are derived from materials provided by the organizations. All have publications or information available for interested readers. The list was compiled on the date of publication of the present volume; the information provided here may change. Be aware that many organizations take several weeks or longer to respond to inquiries, so allow as much time as possible.

American Enterprise Institute (AEI)
1150 Seventeenth Street NW, Washington, DC   20036
(202) 862-5800 • fax: (202) 862-7177
Web site: www.aei.org

AEI is a conservative think tank based in Washington, DC. Its members support free trade in Latin America and believe that populism poses a threat to democracy in the region. AEI publishes books such as *Latin America: Dependency or Interdependence?* and the magazine *American Enterprise*, the current issue of which is available on its Web site. The AEI Web site also publishes articles and commentary, including "The End of the Bolivarian Age" and "Chávez Wrecks Venezuela, Democracy."

Amnesty International USA
Five Penn Plaza, New York, NY   10001
(212) 807-8400 • fax: (212) 627-1451
Web site: www.amnestyusa.org

Amnesty International works to ensure that governments do not deny individuals their basic human rights as outlined in the United Nations Universal Declaration of Human Rights. It publishes books, its *State of the World* report, and the quarterly magazine *amnesty*. Recent and archived issues of its magazine and *State of the World* report are available on the Web site.

Brookings Institution

1775 Massachusetts Ave. NW, Washington, DC   20036
(202) 797-6000 • fax: (202) 797-6004
e-mail: brookinfo@brook.edu
Web site: www.brook.edu

Founded in 1927, the Brookings Institution conducts research and analyzes global events and their impact on the United States and U.S. foreign policy. It publishes the quarterly *Brookings Review* and numerous books and research papers on foreign policy. Numerous articles and commentary on Latin America are available on the institution's Web site, including "Latin America: Coming of Age" and "Can Latin American Economies Deflect the Financial Crisis?"

CATO Institute

1000 Massachusetts Ave. NW, Washington, DC   20001-5403
(202) 842-0200 • fax: (202) 842-3490
Web site: www.cato.org

CATO is a libertarian public policy research foundation dedicated to peace and limited government intervention in foreign affairs. It publishes numerous reports and periodicals, including *Policy Analysis* and *Cato Policy Review*, both of which discuss U.S. policy in Latin America. CATO also publishes numerous books, including *Bad Neighbor Policy: Washington's Futile War on Drugs in Latin America*. On its Web site, CATO members publish analysis and commentary supporting free trade and opposing the U.S. war on drugs in Latin America.

Center for Economic and Policy Research (CEPR)

1611 Connecticut Ave. NW, Suite 400
Washington, DC   20009
(202) 293-5380 • fax: (202) 588-1356

e-mail: cepr@cepr.net
Web site: www.cepr.net

CEPR is a liberal think tank that reports on political and economic issues in Latin America. The center believes that for citizens to effectively exercise their voices in a democracy, they should be informed about the problems and choices that they face. Thus, CEPR conducts research and public education to allow broad segments of the public to know exactly what is at stake in major policy debates. On its Web site, the center publishes lectures, testimony, and commentary, including "South America: Recession Can Be Avoided" and the reports *Argentina: The Crisis That Isn't* and *Poverty Reduction in Venezuela: A Reality Based View.*

Center for Strategic and International Studies (CSIS)
1800 K St. NW, Washington, DC 20006
(202) 887-0200 • fax: (202) 775-3199
Web site: www.csis.org

CSIS is a public policy research institution that specializes in U.S. domestic and foreign policy, national security, and economic policy. The center's Americas Program focuses on examining key issues in the region, such as political party development, the administration of justice and rule of law, elections and electoral reform, anti-corruption measures and transparency, and international cooperation in support of democracy. Its publications include the journal *The Washington Quarterly,* the monthly *Hemisphere Highlights,* and the periodic newsletter *Hemisphere Focus.* Recent and archived issues of these publications are available on its Web site. CSIS also publishes reports and policy papers, including *Anticorruption Efforts in Latin America: Lessons Learned* and *Judicial Reform in Latin America.*

Council on Foreign Relations (CFR)
58 E. Sixty-Eighth St., New York, NY 10021
(212) 434-9400 • fax: (212) 986-2984
Web site: www.cfr.org

The council specializes in foreign affairs and studies the international aspects of American political and economic policies and problems. Its journal *Foreign Affairs*, published five times a year, includes analyses of current conflicts around the world. Reports, articles, and commentary by CFR members are available on its Web site, including the CFR task force report *U.S.-Latin America Relations: A New Direction for a New Reality*, the backgrounder article "Venezuela's Oil-Based Economy," and the op-ed article "Argentina: Legacy of Skin-Deep Reform."

Council on Hemispheric Affairs (COHA)

1250 Connecticut Ave. N.W., Suite 1C
Washington, DC 20036
(202) 223-4975 • fax: (202) 223-4979
e-mail: coha@coha.org
Web site: www.coha.org

COHA's goal is to increase the importance of the inter-American relationship and encourage the formulation of rational and constructive U.S. policies towards Latin America. COHA condemns Washington's policy towards Cuba and Venezuela, the negative impact of neo-liberal reforms on the average Latin American, and NAFTA (North American Free Trade Agreement) until basic Mexican institutions are truly democratic and trade unions are free enough to negotiate as equals. It publishes the bi-monthly *Washington Report on the Hemisphere* and commentary, reports, and news briefs, including the articles "Still on the Drawing Board: The Banco del Sur a Half Year Later" and "Evaluating Structural Adjustment: A Dissenting Opinion" and the reports *Colombia's Indigenous March for Justice* and *El Salvador: A Deeply Divided Country*, which are available on its Web site.

Heritage Foundation

214 Massachusetts Ave. NE, Washington, DC 20002-4999
(800) 544-4843 • fax: (202) 544-6979
e-mail: pubs@heritage.org
Web site: www.heritage.org

The Heritage Foundation is a public policy research institute that advocates limited government and the free-market system. The foundation publishes the quarterly *Policy Review* as well as monographs, books, and papers on U.S. foreign policy in Latin America, including "Averting Disaster in Argentina: The Case for Economic Freedom," "Chávez, Venezuela, and Russia: A New Cuban Missile Crisis?" and "Rethinking the Summit of the Americas and Advancing Free Trade in Latin America," which are available on its Web site.

Human Rights Watch

350 Fifth Ave., 34th Fl., New York, NY 10118-3299
(212) 290-4700
e-mail: hrwnyc@hrw.org
Web site: www.hrw.org

Founded in 1978, Human Rights Watch conducts systematic investigations of human rights abuses in countries around the world, including those in Latin America. It publishes many books and reports on specific countries and issues, as well as annual reports, recent selections of which are available on its Web site. On its "Americas" link, Human Rights Watch includes news and commentary on current human-rights issues in Latin America, such as "Colombia: Not Time for a Trade Deal," "Nicaragua: Protect Rights Advocates from Harassment and Intimidation," and "A Decade Under Chávez."

Inter-American Dialogue

1211 Connecticut Ave. NW, Suite 510
Washington, DC 20036
(202) 822-9002 • fax: (202) 822-9553
Web site: www.thedialogue.org

Comprised of public and private leaders from across the Americas, Inter-American Dialogue addresses hemispheric problems and promotes opportunities. The organization seeks to build cooperation among Western Hemisphere nations and advance democratic governance, social equity, and economic growth. It publishes the monthly newsletter *Dialogue/Dialogo* and the *Latin America Advisor* newsletter, recent issues of which are available on its Web site.

Latin American and Caribbean Center (LACC)

Florida International University, University Park, DM 353
Miami, FL 33199
(305) 348-2894 • fax: (305) 348-3593
e-mail: lacc@fiu.edu
Web site: http://lacc.fiu.edu

Founded in 1979, LACC is a federally funded resource center for Latin American and Caribbean studies in partnership with the University of Florida's Center for Latin American Studies. Scholars produce work on migration, U.S.-Latin American relations, trade and integration in the Americas, indigenous cultures, economic stabilization and democratization, sustainable development, environmental technology, and arts and humanities. LACC publishes the twice-yearly magazine *Hemisphere* and the periodic *Journal of Latin American Anthropology*. Abstracts of current research are available on the LACC Web site.

North American Congress on Latin America (NACLA)

38 Greene St., 4th Floor, New York, NY 10013
(646) 613-1440 • fax: (646) 613-1443
Web site: http://nacla.org

Founded in 1966, NACLA's goal is to free the nations and peoples of Latin America and the Caribbean from oppression and injustice. It promotes a relationship with the United States that is based on mutual respect and free from economic and political subordination. NACLA publishes books, produces radio programs on Latin American affairs and U.S. Policy, and hosts an Internet resource center of news and information from Latin America. The organization also publishes *NACLA Report on the Americas*, a bi-monthly magazine of news and analysis, recent issues of which are available on its Web site.

Magazine articles include, "Guns: The Small Arms Trade in the Americas" and "Putting Down Roots: The Latin American Right Today."

U.S. Department of State

2201 C St. NW, Washington, DC   20520
(202) 647-4000
Web site: www.state.gov

The U.S. State Department is a federal agency that advises the president on the formulation and execution of foreign policy. Its Bureau of Western Hemisphere Affairs works with partners in the Americas to generate broad-based growth through freer trade and sound economic policies, to invest in the well-being of all Latin America peoples, and to make democracy serve every citizen more effectively and justly. Information on the Pathways to Prosperity in the Americas Initiative, the goal of which is to promote free trade and open investment, and the Merida Initiative, the goal of which is to confront criminal organizations in Latin America, are available on its Web site, as are links to regional topics on CAFTA (Central America Free Trade Agreement), Cuba, and other regional initiatives.

Washington Office on Latin America (WOLA)

1666 Connecticut Ave. NW, Suite 400
Washington, DC   20009
(202) 797-2171 • fax: (202) 797-2172
Web site: www.wola.org

WOLA was founded in 1974 by a coalition of civic and religious leaders. Its mission is to promote human rights, democracy, and social and economic justice in Latin America and the Caribbean. WOLA monitors the impact of policies and programs of governments and international organizations and recommends alternatives through reporting, education, training, and advocacy. Its Web site publishes news and articles, including "New Report on Violence and Judicial Corruption in Central America," "The Promise and the Perils of Agricultural

Trade Liberalization: Lessons from Latin America," and "The Coca Debate: Headed toward Polarization or Common Ground?"

Bibliography of Books

Roberto Regalado Álvarez — *Latin America at the Crossroads: Domination, Crisis, Popular Movements, and Political Alternatives.* Melbourne, Australia: Ocean Press, 2007.

Daniel M. Brinks — *The Judicial Response to Police Killing in Latin America.* New York: Cambridge University Press, 2008.

David V. Carruthers, ed. — *Environmental Justice in Latin America.* Cambridge: MIT Press, 2008.

Edward L. Cleary — *Mobilizing for Human Rights in Latin America.* Bloomfield, CT: Kumarian Press, 2007.

Vittorio Corbo and Andrea Tokman — *Latin America in a Global World: Challenges Ahead.* Santiago: Banco Central de Chile, 2007.

Michaelene Cox, ed. — *State of Corruption, State of Chaos: The Terror of Political Malfeasance.* Lanham, MD: Lexington Books, 2008.

Juanita Darling — *Latin America, Media, and Revolution: Communication in Modern Mesoamerica.* New York: Palgrave Macmillan, 2008.

Peter DeShazo, Tanya Primiani, and Phillip McLean — *Back from the Brink: Evaluating Progress in Colombia, 1999–2007.* Washington, DC: CSIS Press, 2007.

Esteban Morales Dominguez and Gary Prevost
United States-Cuban Relations: A Critical History. Lanham, MD: Lexington Books, 2008.

Steven S. Dudley
Walking Ghosts: Murder and Guerrilla Politics in Colombia. New York: Routledge, 2004.

Richard Gott
Guerrilla Movements in Latin America. New York: Seagull Books, 2008.

Ricardo Gottschalk and Patricia Justino, eds.
Overcoming Inequality in Latin America: Issues and Challenges for the Twenty-First Century. New York: Routledge, 2006.

Greg Grandin
Empire's Workshop: Latin America, the United States, and the Rise of the New Imperialism. New York: Macmillan, 2006.

Alexander I. Gray and Antoni Kapcia, eds.
The Changing Dynamic of Cuban Civil Society. Gainesville: University Press of Florida, 2008.

Jerry Haar and John Price, eds.
Can Latin America Compete? Confronting the Challenges of Globalization. New York: Palgrave Macmillan, 2008.

Henry Heller
The Cold War and the New Imperialism: A Global History. New York: Monthly Review Press, 2006.

Irving Louise Horowitz
The Long Night of Dark Intent: A Half Century of Cuban Communism. New Brunswick, NJ: Transaction, 2008.

Gilbert M. Joseph and Daniela Spenser — *In from the Cold: Latin America's New Encounter with the Cold War.* Durham, NC: Duke University Press, 2008.

Benjamin Keen and Keith Haynes — *A History of Latin America.* Boston: Houghton Mifflin Harcourt, 2009.

Paul H. Lewis — *Authoritarian Regimes in Latin America: Dictators, Despots, and Tyrants.* Lanham, MD: Rowman & Littlefield, 2006.

Fernando López-Alves and Diane E. Johnson — *Globalization and Uncertainty in Latin America.* New York: Palgrave Macmillan, 2007.

Eduardo Lora, ed. — *The State of State Reform in Latin America.* Stanford, CA: Stanford University Press, 2007.

Gabriel Marcella — *American Grand Strategy for Latin America in the Age of Resentment.* Carlisle, PA: Strategic Studies Institute, U.S. Army War College, 2007.

Alan McPherson, ed. — *Anti-Americanism in Latin America and the Caribbean.* New York: Berghahn Books, 2006.

Alan McPherson, ed. — *Intimate Ties, Bitter Struggles: The United States and Latin America Since 1945.* Washington, DC: Potomac Books, 2006.

Gerardo L. Munck, ed. — *Regimes and Democracy in Latin America: Theories and Methods.* New York: Oxford University Press, 2007.

Gary Prevost and Carlos Oliva Campos, eds. *The Bush Doctrine and Latin America.* New York: Palgrave Macmillan, 2007.

D. L. Raby *Democracy and Revolution: Latin America and Socialism Today.* Toronto: Between the Lines, 2006.

Sybil Rhodes *Social Movements and Free-Market Capitalism in Latin America: Telecommunications Privatization and the Rise of Consumer Protest.* Albany: State University of New York Press, 2006.

James Francis Rochlin *Social Forces and the Revolution in Military Affairs: The Cases of Colombia and Mexico.* New York: Palgrave Macmillan, 2007.

Manuel Alcántara Sáez, ed. *Politicians and Politics in Latin America.* Boulder, CO: Lynne Rienner Publishers, 2008.

Javier Santiso *Latin America's Political Economy of the Possible: Beyond Good Revolutionaries and Free-Marketeers.* Cambridge: MIT Press, 2006.

Javier Santiso *The Visible Hand of China in Latin America.* Paris: Development Centre of the Organisation for Economic Co-Operation and Development, 2007.

Andrés Solimano   *Vanishing Growth in Latin America: The Late Twentieth Century Experience.* Northampton, MA: Edward Elgar, 2006.

Isabel Studer and Carol Wise, eds.   *Requiem or Revival? The Promise of North American Integration.* Washington, DC: Brookings Institution Press, 2007.

Kimberley L. Thachuck, ed.   *Transnational Threats: Smuggling and Trafficking in Arms, Drugs, and Human Life.* Westport, CT: Praeger Security International, 2007.

Harry E. Vanden and Gary Prevost   *Politics of Latin America: The Power Game.* New York: Oxford University Press, 2009.

Robert Clifford Williamson   *Latin America: Cultures in Conflict.* New York: Palgrave Macmillan, 2006.

Thomas C. Wright   *State Terrorism in Latin America: Chile, Argentina, and International Human Rights.* Lanham, MD: Rowman & Littlefield, 2007.

Index